While every precaution has been taken in the preparation of this book, the publisher assumes no responsibility for errors or omissions, or for damages resulting from the use of the information contained herein.

ANXIETY & DEPRESSION IN CHILDREN & TEENS

First edition. December 7, 2022.

Copyright © 2022 Anne C Galloway.

ISBN: 979-8215062142

Written by Anne C Galloway.

ANXIETY AND DEPRESSION IN CHILDREN AND TEENS

INTRODUCTION

Adolescents, particularly early teenagers, have daily anxiety-inducing issues. Indeed, many children and teenagers are more prone to anxiety and panic attacks than most adults.

With the pressures of academic achievement, biological changes in the body, changes in their social lives and the impending arrival of adulthood, teens often have a harder time coping with many of the disturbing situations presented to them in today's world.

Compared to most adults, because they lack the skills associated with maturity, teens often have a harder time coping with many of the disturbing situations presented to them in today's world.

Youngsters whose parents urge them to work harder as they approach the end of their school years to earn the grades required for admission to reputed universities. While urging children to work more, some parents even encourage them to consider the future and start a family.

Consider that these pressures may be sufficient to cause some teens to doubt themselves, resulting in sleepless nights and intense feelings of uneasiness. While anxiety in teenagers is often a natural reaction to many of their daily activities (going on dates, sitting for examinations, meeting new people, participating in sports, performing on stage), other teens feel anxiety in unique ways.

As with anxiety symptoms in toddlers, teens might experience extreme worry simply by thinking about future events. When they do, these episodes often trigger illogical concerns that manifest as terrible panic attacks.

Some teenagers exhibit an irrational reaction to everyday situations and appear to be hypersensitive. This does not necessarily indicate they are anxious but if you are concerned about your child's restlessness, lack of food, social withdrawal, difficulty concentrating or unexpected outbursts of rage, schedule time to sit with them and have a calm conversation.

Often, simply letting them know you're there for them and prepared to support them regardless of what's going on in their lives is all they need.

Under normal conditions, every teenager will experience anxiety due to anything specific occurring in their lives from time to time. However, remember that there is a clear distinction between the normal worry that a healthy child experiences daily and the unreasonable crippling dread that a child with an anxiety or panic attack problem has.

Often, teens who are filled with insecurities, low self-esteem and depression will turn to external sources for relief, which is usually when drugs, alcohol and sexual promiscuity come into play - and, as the pressures mount, these same teens will do anything to alleviate the anxiety, with some even contemplating suicide.

In any given situation, a teenager's reaction may be quite different from another's and hence there is no universal set of symptoms. Nonetheless, most teens who experience anxiety or panic attacks will exhibit at least some of the following symptoms: shortness of breath, chest pain, heartburn, hyperactivity, palpitations, smothering sensations, sweating or shivering, numbness in the head or face, stomach pains and, in severe cases, fear of going insane.

Medical, psychological or physical disorders can cause many of the symptoms mentioned above. Also, they may be the result of an underlying medical condition or treatment, a side effect of some medications or the body's natural response to intense stimuli. Consider this before jumping to conclusions and if you continue to have doubts, consult your physician.

Adolescents and children in their early twenties are more likely than 20 years ago to developmental disorders. Even though less than one in ten adults today suffers from an anxiety disorder, the harsh reality is that up to 20% of 12- to 16-year-olds will develop a mental health disorder and one in four of these children is at risk of developing a severe disorder and that girls, in particular, report more anxiety disorders than boys.

Also, it was discovered that frequent occurrences of anxiety in adolescents significantly impair their ability to manage different daily activities: relationships with young friends; social competence; and academic success and if left untreated, these anxieties can develop into a chronic disorder in adulthood and some cases, clinical depression, which can lead to suicidal thoughts.

Each child suffers some type of anxiety during their early development. Typically, anxiety is triggered by everyday fears: fear of the dark, fear of attending school for the first time, fear of being alone.

Most children eventually learn to manage with and overcome these worries as part of their growth. Still, when anxiety symptoms in children are ignored or misinterpreted, the worry often hinders them from enjoying the typical day-to-day experience of being young and alive.

Happy Reading

CHAPTER 1

Children's Depression

There are many reasons for depression. As a result, it can't be limited to a set age. Disruption of a child's usual pattern of behavior is common when depression is persistent in youngsters as young as five years old.

Depression does not just affect adults; it also affects children. Depression in children can be addressed with medication and therapy strategies. When a child's depression symptoms persist and impair the child's normal conduct, the child is deemed depressed.

Children are extremely sensitive and their degree of depression or risk of depression is fairly high, especially when they suffer a sudden loss or are unable to study or pay attention to some task. Depression in children and adolescents is often inherited, affecting youngsters whose family has a long history of the disorder.

Suppose you notice your child withdrawing from typical everyday activities or displaying signs of melancholy, boredom or low self-esteem. In such instance, you should consult a doctor immediately, as these are all symptoms of depression. A child is an ineffective communicator.

There are many things that your child may like to convey but is unable to. Occasionally, they will attempt suicide or engage in other self-destructive conduct. Therefore, if you see any such significant change in his or her conduct, you should seek quick medical attention to determine the main cause of the problem.

Depression at such a young age is undesirable. One in every five adolescents suffers from depression and the causes are fairly unpredictable. Given the sensitive nature of the adolescent years, parents need to monitor their children rather than allow them to live their lives as they like.

In children and adolescents, an abrupt change in mood, appetite or weight is one of the primary causes of depression. Typically, they demonstrate a lack of enthusiasm in their daily tasks. The unexpected death of a close relative or friend might exacerbate the condition of despair.

The problem becomes more serious when these impressionable brains begin to blame themselves for the current state of affairs and it is at this point, one should exercise extreme caution. They often withdraw from the social world and live in their universe, anything but normal.

Depression in children and adolescents can be fatal and medical and professional assistance should be sought immediately. Early treatment of depression ensures a rapid recovery; otherwise, the problem

deteriorates with time. Assist these young minds in reclaiming their lives by demonstrating your concern.

Depression in adolescent boys often manifests itself in aggressive behavior or other activities deemed unacceptable by society or the law. Among females, self-destructive conduct and suicide ideation are prevalent.

It's natural for parents to be upset and perhaps angered by their children's activities. However, this exacerbates the condition. Parents should be aware that assistance is accessible and that there is no harm in visiting a medical professional to treat depression.

Comparing Female and Male Depression

Before puberty, it is generally considered that gender has little, if any, effect on the level of depression in girls and boys. However, as females enter puberty, their depression levels skyrocket and they may get the most severe form of depression, Major Depressive Disorder. This is unknown but related to the hormonal, physical and emotional changes that girls undergo as they mature into adults.

Female Depression

• As youngsters mature into adolescents, both sexes should begin to recognize their worth in society. Boys learn that girls face societal and emotional constraints about their behavior.

As a result, boys develop a sense of superiority over their female counterparts. On the other hand, girls may suffer from inferiority complexes and low self-esteem and feel worthless and ineffective. These particular girls are predisposed to depression.

• During puberty, girls developed an increased concern for their physical appearance, a concern not often shared by boys of the same age. Also, girls are more influenced by weight gain than boys are throughout the development of secondary sexual traits.

• Adolescent females are more important of themselves for what they perceive to be sexual offenses. For instance, society views a female adolescent with multiple premarital sex partners as more immoral than a male adolescent with a comparable number of partners. This burdens the girls and they often exhibit depressive symptoms as a result.

• In comparison to males, females are more likely to acquire depression due to perceived sexual undesirability. Thus, if a teenage girl believes she falls short of the beauty ideal, she may feel perpetually depressed, withdrawn, anxious and helpless despite reassurance.

• Adjustment disorder with a sad mood is more common in girls than in boys, perhaps because they hit puberty sooner and the transition to high school is more difficult for girls than for males.

• As girls interact with guys, they engage in cooperative communication while the boys engage in domineering communication, establishing the girls as contributors and the boys as decision-makers. This leads to girls' sense of insignificance, utility and uncertainty in social situations. This is a significant contributor to depression in susceptible girls.

• Girls often exhibit tearfulness, withdrawal, self-mutilation, sleeping and eating disorders and are likely to act out sexually in response to depression. In comparison to male colleagues, this is not the case.

Boys Suffer From Depression

Before puberty, boys experience the same level of depression as females but become less sensitive when they enter puberty. They face less stress and have fewer duties than their male colleagues. The following are the most prevalent signs of depression in boys:

• Boys are assertive and often express their despair through anger, impatience and other temperamental characteristics that often land them in hot water. Thus, males who consistently demonstrate hostility and disobedience toward authority figures should be evaluated for childhood or adolescent depression.

• When boys are depressed, they develop addicted behaviors. They often engage in substance abuse when they are unhappy, believing that the substances would help them overcome their depression. If a teenager adopts these habits unexpectedly, parents should investigate the source, as these teenage guys are more likely to be suffering from melancholy, anxiety or both.

• Depressed males are more prone to avoid school, shun social meetings and express pessimism. While their reactions are less severe than females, they are more likely to get into trouble.

• Boys may become violent, severing links to family, friends, peers and authorities, including instructors. While most females will bow to authority figures and respond with shyness and withdrawal, males act violently.

What Distinction Does Adolescent Depression Have From Adult Depression?

Depressive symptoms are widespread and most people will experience them without being labeled as depression. The lifetime prevalence of depression varies between 5% and 12% for males and 10% to 25% for women. In 1990, major depression was placed fourth in terms of disease burden, dysfunction and risk factors.

Depression is linked with an increased risk of cancer, cardiovascular illness, immunological dysfunction, allergies, migraine, anxiety, infectious disease and suicide.

The body reacts similarly to depression and stress. Corticosteroids are hormones that are released when an individual is stressed or depressed. Cortisol levels produced by the adrenal glands are elevated and sustained during the depression, impairing long-term memory.

Individuals with depression also have increased activity in their hypothalamus, pituitary gland and adrenal glands. A decrease in the volume of the hypothalamus has been observed in response to chronic stress.

The hypothalamus processes signal from the autonomic nervous system and are involved in feeding, sexual behavior, sleep patterns, emotions and hormone secretion. Individuals who have experienced many episodes of depression exhibit aberrant electroencephalogram sleep patterns. Enlarged ventricles and increased cortical atrophy have been observed in depressed patients with psychotic characteristics.

Adolescents may experience depression in different ways. Adolescents and youngsters, according to the DSM-IV-TR, exhibit increased irritability, social disengagement and somatic complaints. Adolescents do not exhibit the same levels of melancholy and psychomotor slowness as adults who exhibit symptoms of depression.

Other than that, adolescent depression might be characterized by rage, disorientation, exhaustion and a loss of enjoyment from ordinarily rewarding activities. Another characteristic of adolescent depression is that it is equally prevalent in males and females.

Due to the symptoms associated with adolescent depression, it can be difficult to diagnose. The disease is often co-occurring with other conditions, including Conduct Disorder, Attention-Deficit/Hyperactivity Disorder and Anxiety.

There are two distinct types of depression. Shyness, nervousness, worrying behavior and inhibition are all related to internalizing style. Externalizing behavior is linked to substance misuse and conduct disorder.

Many studies have established a relationship between depression and other psychosocial characteristics and adults' perceptions of pain. As a result, depression or depression-related symptoms would be observed in teenagers who experience pain. In adolescents, low back and mid-back discomfort have been associated with a sense of well-being.

Adolescents and children with back pain regard their health as poor and report being miserable. Physical health is a strong predictor of depression in teenagers, both current and prospective. In general, physical illness is related to depression.

Depression in children and adolescents must be treated as an illness and detected early. It necessitates ongoing medical attention and counseling on both the medical and familial levels.

CHAPTER 2

15

Is Your Child Suffering From Depression and Anxiety?

It's difficult to comprehend that any child may suffer from anxiety or despair. What could create such distress in youngsters at such a young age? They have not encountered the adversity that can precipitate these problems in adults.

The reality is that one in every ten adolescents suffers from an anxiety problem and one in every 33 children develops clinical depression. Unresolved anxiety might develop into depression. One in every eight youngsters is at risk of developing adolescent depression, manifesting in suicidal ideation.

Why are some teenagers more anxious than others? There are many reasons for this, which can be classified as follows:

1. Psychological - When a youngster cannot cope with physical changes and the difficulties of adolescence, they become excessively nervous. This can also be a taught behavior from a close relative. Around 50% of persons who suffer from an anxiety disorder have a family member who suffers from the disease. This brings us to the second reason.

2. Hereditary - Scientists have been unable to determine precisely how much anxiety is a learned response in response to a role model and how much is a genetic predisposition to timidity and worry. However, there is evidence to support the theory that both factors are to blame.

3. Biological - Studies have revealed that persons who suffer from anxiety disorders often exhibit aberrant brain function in some areas of the brain, specifically norepinephrine, serotonin and GABA.

4. Medical - Before diagnosing an anxiety disorder, examinations must rule out the presence of underlying medical diseases such as cardiovascular illness, lung disease, some types of tumors, thyroid problems, infections and neurologic disease.

Every adolescent is concerned about something - school, their beauty, peer approval and their future. However, what constitutes a healthy amount of anxiety and what constitutes an unhealthy level? Probably the greatest criterion to consider is whether anxiety interferes with your child's life to the point where previously ordinary activities have become obsolete.

Consider two factors: physical complaints and behavioral difficulties. Physical symptoms include nausea, sweating, headaches, diarrhea, stomach pains, high blood pressure, and heart palpitations. Out-of-character and undesirable behaviors manifest behavioral disorders.

For instance, are they abstaining from school?

Are they struggling in class?

Are they constantly staying in, although in the past they would socialize with their friends?

Do they believe that if their work or appearance is not flawless, they will be rejected - resulting in obsessive checking and re-checking?

Do you assume they consume alcoholic beverages, smoke or use illegal substances?

Teenagers who suffer from anxiety disorders report being unable to concentrate on academics, having difficulty making decisions and perceiving their environment differently than they used to.

There are six distinct forms of anxiety disorders, not all of which affect children and adolescents. Generalized anxiety disorder (GAD), social anxiety disorder and panic disorder are more prevalent in pre-adolescent and adolescent populations. Depression often coexists with these disorders, particularly in teens.

Notify your child's doctor right away if you suspect an anxiety or depression disorder. Consult a mental health professional who specializes in children's mental health issues.

Different elements come into play when children are engaged, which varies according to their ages, developmental stages, childhood experiences, family history, and other circumstances.

Children cannot be diagnosed using the same diagnostic methods as adults. Typical disorders include mood and emotional disturbances, depression, anxiety disorders, behavioral disorders, and eating disorders.

Counseling, medicine and creative expression therapy are often used as treatment alternatives. This form of treatment assists your youngster in comprehending his or her emotions with thought processes. With sufficient coaching, your child will acquire excellent coping mechanisms for difficult situations, particularly as the adolescent years approach.

Sessions of creativity are good for helping your youngster to express himself and safely discharge pent-up emotions. Also, it enables him to transmit those emotions to others. Group and family therapy are often extremely effective as well, as they assist children in developing the necessary skills for social interaction.

The family needs to be involved directly in their child's treatment. Your involvement is important in assisting and encouraging your child in developing confidence and self-esteem. Confirm your affection for your child by doing so. Assure him that he is accepted as a family member on an equal footing.

Children who feel loved develop a sense of security in themselves and their environment. This substantially contributes to their ability to build coping skills and good relationships.

Acceptance is important for a child, even more so as he enters school, where peers can be cruel and judgmental. A child with a healthy sense of self-worth and confidence can adjust far more quickly and easily than one who feels unworthy.

Make a habit of encouraging and complimenting your child frequently, not only for a job well done but for simply being who he is.

Mention something nice about your child every now and during family chats, whether it's his intelligence, a particular aptitude or a physical advantage such as being strong for his age.

When a child hears such wonderful words stated about him or her, the meaning quickly sinks in and the child develops confident self-confidence. Wherever there is confidence, anxiety disorders and sadness often do not occur.

Early self-confidence development will benefit your child substantially as he approaches his adolescent years and all the associated difficulties. Also, it will provide the necessary tools to prevent teen depression from becoming an issue.

While you cannot change your child's biological or genetic makeup, you can surely influence how he perceives himself as an individual and a member of society.

While independence is emphasized heavily, parents need to remain actively involved in their children's lives, possibly even more so as they enter adolescence. You are responsible for setting limits on what your child watches on television and how immersed he or she becomes in video games.

The Self-Esteem of Your Child and Why It Is Important

Self-esteem is just the worth you place on yourself. Your self-perceived views and concepts, whether true or incorrect. Why is this important for your child's development? A strong foundation in this area will help your child throughout their years, from childhood to the subsequent stages. Self-esteem is a rather accurate indicator of one's mental health.

Healthy self-esteem enables your child to deal with conflict and enables them to resist harmful influences. This concept has been demonstrated to be true through research. A child who can effectively deal with peer pressure will be happier and more secure in his or her skin. A safe and happy child will be confident and loving.

Independence, an important developmental milestone, is facilitated by increased self-esteem and the responsibility of confronting new obstacles. Also, children's capacity to manage both happy and negative emotional sensations is a benefit. When your child is strong and confident, he or she should have an easier time resolving conflicts with siblings and friends.

This steadfastly optimistic approach will benefit your child during whatever transitional stage they may encounter such as moving to a new neighborhood, a new school or new family members are all scenarios that might provide difficulties for most youngsters.

Even something as simple as a new classmate can be a source of anxiety for some children. Healthy self-esteem can be beneficial in any of these scenarios.

This is the basis upon which your child will build. A child that is safe, joyful and confident should have an easier time transitioning into adolescence. The pre-adolescent and adolescent years can be rather perplexing. A youngster who enters this period equipped with the necessary mental and emotional tools has a far better chance of navigating this turbulent phase successfully.

When a youngster has poor self-esteem, he or she may struggle with feelings of uneasiness and anxiety. Also, they may struggle to make friends and exhibit inappropriate behavior. Bringing these concerns into adolescence might result in academic underperformance and even despair.

At every stage of life, self-esteem is important. Having a strong foundation, beginning in childhood, is arguably the most important factor in developing self-esteem.

By implementing these precautions early on and seeking assistance as soon as issues develop, you can have a notable impact on your child's future. You can assist your child in avoiding anxiety disorders and depression, which can cause issues in many areas of his life.

CHAPTER 3

22

Children's Anxiety Disorders

Perhaps it is surprising and sometimes upsetting to learn that children, like adults, can suffer from different anxiety problems. We typically consider childhood a carefree period, the one time in a child's life when they are not concerned with doing a job or assuming property ownership duties.

However, upon reflection, we may realize that a child growing up must face and conquer many obstacles before reaching school-leaving age. Within the first years of life, a small child must adjust to being separated from its mother, learn about potty training, and connect socially with other children.

Once a child reaches primary school age, the educational challenge begins with passing tests, excelling in sports, and being popular among peers. Some amount of tension is natural along the journey.

Even at a relatively young age, we may expect a child to be anxious if they have an upcoming exam or are scheduled to appear in the school play. An anxiety disorder emerges when a youngster worries excessively and exhibits signs of distress or cannot perform normally.

Children with excessive anxiety may exhibit different symptoms, including the inability to sleep or eat correctly, bedwetting, irritability, lack of focus, headaches, stomach problems or nausea or simply an unwillingness to attend school. These are all signs that something is wrong in the child's life and determining the particular problem is not always easy.

To aid in diagnosing and treating anxiety in children, it is categorized as generalized anxiety disorder, panic disorder, separation disorder, social disorder, obsessive-compulsive disorder, and post-traumatic stress disorder. Occasionally, there may be overlap, as when a youngster suffers from general anxiety and panic attacks or general anxiety and specific fear of social activities.

Anxiety in general

This is comparable to what an adult could go through in that the youngster worries excessively about everything and is often depressed and irritated. An anxious child may have difficulty sleeping or performing well in school, which sadly exacerbates the condition. There may be a single identifiable reason, such as being bullied at school, but professional assistance is recommended if none can be identified.

Anxiety Disorder

This is characterized by brief bursts of acute worry and panic that occur repeatedly. Although the attacks often last only a few minutes to a half-hour, they can occur rather often and are extremely disturbing.

Fearful feelings are so severe that they manifest physically as beating heart, shortness of breath or vomiting.

Occasionally, with appropriate parental help, children can overcome these obstacles independently, but they can also result in withdrawal and a lack of desire to socialize. If this occurs or your child is depressed for an extended period, you should consult a physician.

Separation Disturbance

Separation from the mother can be slightly distressing for a child the first time but most children cope well and quickly adjust. However, when a youngster attends school and is apart from his or her mother for the entire day, he or she may exhibit signs of excessive anxiousness. This may manifest as clutching, stomach or headache pain or nightmares. With constant reassurance and assistance, the kid may overcome these phobias in due course.

Social Disturbance

Social dysfunction typically manifests itself during adolescence, when most children are eager to socialize with their classmates. A teenager with social phobia will avoid these activities and will generally be uncomfortable or ashamed to participate. While social phobia may not always interfere with schoolwork, it does impair the normal development of social skills.

OCD is a type of obsessive-compulsive disorder (OCD)

A child with OCD often has obsessive thoughts that they are unable to shake. To divert attention away from these often unpleasant ideas, a youngster would assign himself to conduct a ritual in conjunction with some mundane activity.

Each step must be performed in a specific order or manner. Often, this implies that an excessive amount of time is spent on mundane activities, which wastes time and distracts the youngster.

Distress following a terrible event

A traumatic experience can be particularly harmful to a youngster, resulting in emotional distress that can endure a long time and be difficult to overcome. The symptoms are similar to generalized anxiety, with occasional nightmares, sleep difficulties, appetite loss and an anxious state of mind. Professional assistance may be required to assist a youngster in overcoming these fears.

CHAPTER 4

26

Symptoms Of Anxiety Disorder In Teens And Adolescents

Childhood anxiety ranks high on the list of the most feared events for parents and families. Children, like complex development "sponges," are susceptible to different incoming influences. Other children place significant pressures and choices on your child. Your child is spoon-fed school and a values-based culture.

Could all of this "stuff" be causing uncertainty and fear through repetitive behavior patterns, so precipitating the beginnings of teen anxiety disorders, phobias, drug misuse, obsessive-compulsive disorder, general withdrawal and an antisocial outlook? Yes. It is a serious and present danger for a large number of children.

Physical Symptoms of Teen Anxiety

What parents perceive as "difficult" is insignificant in comparison to the growing nightmare experienced by children. Parents should be aware of the physical symptoms of Bad Guy anxiety, which include breathing difficulties, a raised heart and pulse rate, headaches, dizziness, nausea, sleeping disorders and on-again-off-again eating habits.

Teen Anxiety Depression Symptoms

While the physical insults associated with teen anxiety are a serious concern, the deeper embedded behavioral roots of anxiety depression disorder present a greater and more complicated intervention and treatment challenge.

Symptoms of Obsessive-Compulsive Disorder

Parents cannot be too vigilant in focusing their attention on their children, looking for telltale signs of obsessive-compulsive disorder. A restless and fidgety obsession with minutiae may begin innocently enough with things in some location, fear of dirt and germs or eating disorders such as bulimia.

Antisocial "self-isolating" behavior

Antisocial behavior is increasingly manifesting as a defensive and protective response to growing fears and uncertainties. "Keeping the world out" or isolating herself within the "safety" zone of her bedroom or other secure location becomes her primary concern and obsession.

* Self-Denial - drift into dream state filled with panic attacks of anxiety deeper yet, anxiety sadness develops in your child's psyche, where they begin the process of self-denial, where they abstract themselves in an ongoing process of depersonalization. How does your child feel? As if they're about to go insane as if they've begun to drift away from their very selves

Medication For Teen Anxiety Disorder

Cortisol and other stress hormones and physical and psychological symptoms have drawn millions of unhappy adolescents and their frustrated parents into a new encounter with potent mood-changing psychiatric drugs.

* Major Classifications Of Prescribed Anti-Anxiety Medication.

Although the chemistry is complex, parents should understand the broad strokes of these profound mood-changing anxiety medications, including beta-blockers, antidepressants, mild tranquilizers, selective serotonin reuptake inhibitors, and anticonvulsants benzodiazepines, which are marketed under the brand names Xanax, Valium or Librium.

* Drug Strengths and Areas of Concentration.

These psychiatric medications are entirely focused on potency and neuronal targeting. As with carbon dating, drug strength is quantified in terms of "half-life strengths." Parents must enquire about and understand the drug's basic target range.

* Adverse Effects of Anti-Anxiety Medication.

Serious drugs entail grave risks for the user. While 70% of the user population may experience somewhat gratifying and stabilizing effects, continued drug use predisposes a teen or adult to develop drug dependence. Polite speaks for drug addiction.

Without a months-long, carefully managed program of incremental tapering in usage, withdrawal creates its hell. Meanwhile, children and adults may experience severe withdrawal symptoms, including anxiety, panic attacks, confusion, sleep disorders, eating disorders, weight loss, mental confusion, muscle cramping, and diarrhea.

Non-Prescription Herbal Treatments for Teen Anxiety

Before the advent of modern pharmaceuticals, people relied entirely on plant-based medicines and support networks. Botanicals such as ginseng, rosemary, St. John's Wort and kava have been demonstrated in contemporary British side-by-side research with pharmacy medications to have similar positive intervention potentials, without the bad side effects associated with anxiety disorder medication.

Investigate additional information about teen anxiety disorders and natural approaches to regulating your child's brain health and moods while fostering natural sleep and life cycles.

Because adolescence is characterized by mood swings and angry outbursts followed by tearful withdrawals, it can be hard to determine whether your child is acting normally or if their behavior is symptomatic of a more serious condition.

Often, anxiety disorders in children and adolescents go undiagnosed. This can be a difficult error since very nervous adolescents can develop into excessively anxious adults or, more significantly, the shadow of despair and suicide looms large.

CHAPTER 5

Disorders In Children And Adolescents Are Psychological Disorders

Children and adolescents who are mentally, emotionally, and behaviorally dysfunctional do not have a "disease." Medical professionals and pharmaceutical companies would think "biological" factors cause that child and adolescent disorders. They do not do so.

The true origins of a child or adolescent disorder are "psychological" in nature, not biological. The true causes, in essence, are "selfish reactions."

Child and adolescent problems are deliberate and unintentional "selfish behaviors." Typically, the reactions are directed at the disturbed person's selfish parents' unloving and unkind decisions.

These self-centered reactions account for the underlying causes of diseases such as child and adolescent schizophrenia, depression, anxiety, autism, eating disorders, and attention deficit hyperactivity disorder (ADHD).

Our parents are the most vital and significant figures in our life. When a child's parents choose to be excessively selfish, they are frequently also excessively controlling and abusive.

When a baby is born, they have normally spent nine months inside the womb and has endured daily uncomfortable and traumatic psychological-energetic parent-related experiences. These encounters frequently elicited mental and emotional responses.

In combination with unfavorable agreements made with a preferred parent, these reactions provide the groundwork for dysfunctional behavior patterns and atypical symptoms. This is especially true when the parents' control and abuse are excessive, the child's selfish behaviors are extreme, and the child strongly honors child-parent unfavorable agreements.

Each selfish parent has a subconscious and consistent unpleasant and painful subconscious psychological-energetic effect on his or her young child (to varying degrees) (unborn or born).

Psychological-energetic interaction between parents and children begins spontaneously while the baby is an embryo inside the womb. This is how humans communicate before they reach the age of social language acquisition.

Extremely selfish individuals frequently psychologically "separate" and consciously become unconscious of significant subconscious personal incorrect intentions and choices. Additionally, they are mindful of few or no psychic-energetic communications or agreements that may occur between them and their unborn babies.

If an unborn baby's selfish reactions are excessive, they are likely to appear obvious indications of a serious disease such as autism or infant schizophrenia following birth.

Each significant disorder manifests as a child's reaction to a parent's mental, emotional, energetic (psychic), and frequently, later, physical and/or sexual abuse. The severity of a problem is typically proportional to the degree of abuse that precipitated the child's reaction.

Additionally, the sort of reply may provide insight into the type of abuse encountered. Numerous parents' most persistently harmful activities toward their children or adolescents are psychological, subconscious, and purposefully hidden.

When a child is extremely young, reactions may appear as if the youngster is simply "acting out," rather than reacting to a parent's behavior or to something the parent may be doing incorrectly.

It is safe to assume that when a young child or adolescent behaves destructively or abnormally, the explanation is not that the child or adolescent is suffering from a sickness, a brain chemical imbalance, or is being affected by an environmental pollutant.

The prevalent term "acting out" is a euphemism that absolves distressed children and adolescents of all accountability. Frequently, the parents of problematic children are left out of the dysfunctional equations given by their parents and the medical-psychiatric profession.

This apparent exclusion is a significant component of The Great Cover-Up, which explains why abuse, pain, and reaction continue to recycle in families from generation to generation.

Most parents assert that they are "attempting to love" and "doing their best" for their children. Additionally, they claim parents have no idea why their disturbed child or adolescent continually defends, rebelling, and behaving adversely.

Typically, a disturbed child or adolescent is not the one who started a family's negativity. Children and adolescents who are disturbed react to their parents' selfish, controlling, possessive, violent, abusive (conscious and subconscious) and sexually abusive intentions, attitudes, thoughts, feelings, and acts.

By the time a youngster attains the age of two or three, he or she has acquired strong selfish behavior patterns toward his or her parents. Young children who act out are almost certainly reacting to their parents' selfish conscious and subconscious attitudes at the moment. In contrast, a teenager who acts out is almost certainly reacting to an accumulation of unpleasant parental experiences.

If the parents of disturbed children or adolescents dropped (abandoned) their subconscious and conscious selfish, defiant, oppressive, and inappropriate attitudes and behaviors, their disturbed children and adolescents would likely do the same (acting-out). However, convincing a disturbed kid or teen that their parents have chosen to change in true, truly positive, permanent, and selfless ways would almost certainly need a concerted and sustained effort on their part.

It might be quite difficult for a selfish parent to accept and confess that they were the primary initiator of their disturbed child's or teen's destructive behavior.

Adult egos and a person's fabricated favorable image are significant obstacles to overcome. Selfish parents justify their selfish goals, thoughts, feelings, behaviors, and reactions with numerous justifications and excuses.

Children and adolescents who are reactive do the same thing. Our justifications and excuses for reactive choices we did not make often devolve parent-child relationships into unpleasant and fruitless confrontations.

Extremely self-centered parents frequently exhibit subtle attitudes of ownership toward their children. That mindset alone can be the catalyst for a great deal of revolt and response. The dominating, possessive intents exert unpleasant pressure on and badly affect a kid or adolescent.

Those harmful psychic impulses were almost certainly present even when the child was in the womb. Infants, particularly small children, are profoundly affected by their parents' selfish goals, ideas, attitudes, and behaviors.

When parents prioritize their desires over their child's needs, a child would feel abandoned and insecure. No matter how young, a child understands when their parents exert control and seek to dominate them. Regardless of what a youngster may hear to the contrary, he or she is aware of a parent's choice to love or not to love.

CHAPTER 6

36

Symptoms And Signs Of Adolescent Depression

Teenagers are experiencing the most hormonal phase of their lives thus far. This is why so many teenagers are perpetually moody and emotional and often unable to articulate their frustrations, happiness, perplexity, and other emotions. For some teenagers, though, it becomes more than an emotional roller coaster ride.

For some adolescents, depression may overwhelm and obliterate whatever other emotional upheaval the adolescent is experiencing. There are diverse reasons why a teen may be depressed. Fortunately, there are other treatments available for teen depression.

Depression is often defined as an extended period of sadness and despair. There are several reasons why a teen may be experiencing teen depression, including an inability to cope with daily stresses such as maintaining good grades in school, struggling with learning, struggling with relationships, issues with social status and peers, peer pressure to use drugs or alcohol and so on.

Some teenagers may also struggle with bullying, coming to terms with their sexual orientation and other issues. Occasionally, adolescent depression is caused by environmental stress, such as what is going on around them.

If the teen is experiencing family difficulties or is coping with their parent's divorce, the death or absence of a parent, all these factors can affect what is wrong with the teen, perhaps leading to teen depression.

There are many techniques to monitor your kid's behavior to determine if they are exhibiting symptoms of teen depression. Many adolescents and even youngsters who suffer from depression sleep excessively or have difficulty sleeping.

Also, they are prone to demonstrate changes in their dietary habits and may engage in risky behaviors such as drinking, drug use and theft. Bear in mind that not all adolescents with depression exhibit all these symptoms but if someone exhibits a significant number of them for an extended length of time.

- Concentration difficulties
- Apathy Fatigue
- Unexplained ailments such as headaches, back pain and so on.
- Irresponsible conduct
- Loss of memory
- Disobedient behavior
- Sadness
- Anxiety
- A sense of despair
- Gaining or Losing Weight
- Withdrawal from acquaintances
- Grade reductions
- Suicidal thoughts
- Cuts, burns and self-mutilation are all harmful practices.

Treatment options for adolescent depression include the following:

Once an adolescent has been diagnosed by a physician, clinical therapist or psychologist, it is important that they immediately begin therapy. Some youths may resort to self-mutilation or even suicide if therapy is not sought in the most extreme cases. Unfortunately, most depressed adolescents and adults do not seek treatment.

This is why it is important for parents, instructors and friends of teenagers to be aware of the symptoms of teen depression to assist in obtaining treatment for their loved one as soon as possible and avoiding such severe circumstances as suicide. Treatment is available in different formats.

Therapy and support groups can be an excellent approach for some kids to deal with teen depression. Some adolescents may require intensive counseling, while others may benefit from support groups. Other adolescents may be uncomfortable with either option and may prefer to begin therapy with antidepressants or anti-anxiety medication.

Some kids may benefit most from a combination of counseling and medication during their rehabilitation journey. Antidepressants, on the other hand, must be taken and recommended with discretion, particularly in adolescents.

According to the FDA, some antidepressant medications may increase the risk of suicide and suicidal ideation in adolescents and children who suffer from depression or other psychiatric disorders such as bipolar or manic depression.

If a teen is bipolar, they may exhibit similar symptoms to those of depression. Still, they must be treated with a completely different type of medication or risk increasing their risk of suicide.

Unfortunately, each year, approximately 500,000 adolescents attempt suicide and approximately 5,000 succeed. Because these numbers have reached epidemic proportions, preventative measures for parents, teens and peers of at-risk teens must be increased to an all-time high.

CHAPTER 7

Stress and Adolescents

Consider for a moment what you were like in your adolescent years. Have you ever experienced anxiety or stress?

They are in a transition state during their adolescent years, between being a child and desiring to be an autonomous adult. Not only are the adolescent years difficult for parents, they are also difficult for the teenager. It's not an easy time and the stress experienced may be different than that of an adult but it's very real and must be addressed before it spirals out of control.

Each generation faces distinct challenges. For some, growing up during a war was a formative experience. Vietnam and "free love" dominated the 1960s. ASSISTS and drugs were prevalent in the 1980s and 1990s. Now, in 2021, we're coping with a slew of issues and stress has become even more pervasive.

As a child enters their adolescence, they begin the process of self-discovery. They desire to have their voice and thoughts and now they must contend with peer pressure, social pressure and parental pressure.

Having had two children who are now adults with their children and will experience those years with them, I understand how difficult the adolescent years can be for parents.

Teenagers suffer stress, so if you have a teen and have difficulty as a parent or caregiver, educate yourself on handling problems and communicating effectively. Each child will experience this era of growth uniquely. Don't classify your child as good, bad or unique; simply pay attention to see whether they're getting into trouble with something.

Today, if adolescents can tap into their emotions and identify what triggers them, it may help them and their parents communicate more effectively. It is impossible to stress the value of open communication. Teens frequently face the following difficulties:

• The pressures associated with maintaining a good grade in school and gaining admission to the college

• Living up to extremely high standards set by society and family members

• Gang-related violence

• Substance abuse and alcoholism

• Sexual relationships and sexual activity between opposite sexes

• School-related violence and/or bullying

• Abuse - sexual, physical and psychological

• Economical. If they are aware that their parents are anxious about money, this tension is transferred to them.

• And a lot more

Many of these points may sound familiar. They are stressors that teens have faced generation after generation. The economy might be difficult. It's a reality for some parents. When parents lose their employment and cannot provide food or shelter over their heads, it directly affects their children.

When a youngster reaches his or her adolescent years, he or she begins to change. Girls go through hormonal changes, and boys go through puberty and parents may feel the urge to scream and shout at times, believing that their children are the only ones who behave this way. Not true! Most parents will face this issue at some point throughout their children's adolescent years.

Teenagers cannot often manage their emotions and as a result, they become upset, argue with their parents and even lash out in any manner they can. It may take the form of verbal alterations with parents, hanging out with the wrong crowd at school, abusing drugs or alcohol or succumbing to depression.

Never believe that these things will never happen to your child. Socioeconomic status makes no impact when it comes to addiction. When parents have more money, things get worse because it's easier to get their hands on what they wish.

Each of these difficulties can be a ticking time bomb, which is why parents need to learn how to communicate without shouting, threatening or abusing their children in any way. While there are no hard and fast rules for dealing with a worried teenager, the teen's well-being needs to educate oneself on handling various scenarios.

The primary objective is to assist them in recognizing and managing stress in a healthy manner that does not adversely affect their health or future. Among them are the following:

- Maintain open lines of communication regardless of the subject
- Develop the ability to remain calm in the face of adversity
- Spend time as a family having fun—see a movie, go for coffee or go shopping.
- Make a point of sharing a meal with the entire family at least once a week.
- Encourage the adolescent to speak with a counselor
- Also, parents can benefit from speaking with a professional.
- Be conscious of your teen's physical and personality changes.

Stress does not manifest itself in your teen overnight and it does not manifest itself in the same manner in every teenager. Communication and interest are critical to spotting changes that indicate stress or anxiety.

As a parent or caregiver, it is essential to develop coping skills with children of any age so that your life does not become a nightmare throughout the difficult adolescent years.

CHAPTER 8

44

Is Your Teen a Victim of Bullying?

We have all heard about the recent focus on "bullying." While some may be tired of hearing about it, as parents, we must be vigilant. Too many parents are unaware of the extent of their child's suffering until it is too late.

We must increase our awareness of and response to this problem as soon as it is identified. Also, we must be able to spot bullying. I hope you find the information on bullying in the following sections useful and interesting.

Bullying is intentional aggressive behavior characterized by an imbalance of power or strength. It is often repeated throughout time. A bullied child has a difficult time defending himself or herself. According to the American Academy of Child & Adolescent Psychiatry, almost half of all school-aged children are bullied at some point.

Bullying Comes in Four Forms:

1. Physical - striking, shoving, kicking and stealing/damaging property

2. Verbal - slurs, taunts, insults and sexual remarks

3. Emotional - shunned, spread rumors and encourage others to reject or exclude someone

4. Cyber-harassment or intimidation - any form of harassment or intimidation that occurs online

Bullying is most prevalent among students in the fifth, sixth and seventh grades and boys are more likely to be involved than girls.

Boys are very prone to engage in physical and verbal bullying, whereas girls engage in emotional bullying. Typically, boys are bullied by other boys. Both males and females often bully girls.

Possible symptoms that your teen is being bullied include the following:

• Often misplaced or destroyed property

- Avoidance of school-related activities
- Bruises, scrapes and cuts that are unexplained
- is afflicted by headaches/stomachaches
- arriving at school extremely late or extremely early
- looks gloomy, unhappy, moody, tearful or even suicidal
- Apprehension, poor self-esteem
- is displeased upon their return

If you have reason to believe that Cyber Bullying is occurring, make sure to monitor your teen's text messages, Facebook, MySpace and e-mail for the content and context of messages. Checking is not intended to be snooping but rather a technique to ensure that the information your kid receives is suitable and does not involve bullying. (However, I believe that monitoring a teen's technological communications is necessary.)

How you can assist your adolescent:

- Communicate with your adolescent; listen to your adolescent. Your adolescent may be ashamed to tell you if they have been bullied. The courage of a child to tell you if someone is bullying them is admirable.

- Have faith in your adolescent. Teens do not often lie about bullying, so believe your kid. Pay attention to what they're saying. Make no mistake, and this is not a case of "kids will be kids." You must encourage and assist your teen.

- Encourage your adolescent. Propose and role-play techniques to respond assertively without demonstrating aggressive conduct. Have they warned the bully to "shut up or I'm going to report you"? Occasionally, the threat of getting into trouble will bring it to a halt.

- Make contact with the school. While most teenagers may resist your engagement with the school, the school should be aware of your child being threatened at school. Locate someone at your school who will listen to you and is willing to assist you. . Avoid making things worse by ensuring that you have the necessary resources at your disposal.

Most schools now have anti-bullying policies in place, which you can typically locate and study online. If you do not receive a favorable reaction, seek out another candidate; go all the way to the top if necessary. You are your child's advocate and your child has a right to feel secure and be safe at school.

• Encourage your adolescent to socialize. Teens who form groups of two or more have a lower risk of being bullied.

Too many children and adolescents are in distress. Too many young people are in such pain that taking severe measures is their only alternative. Their lives are just getting started. There is much more to life than this particular period when others are subjected to this heinous and terrible treatment.

They are simply too young to comprehend that this is only a brief point in time and that when it occurs, it feels interminable and becomes painful. We are all accountable for instilling in our children a sense of tolerance and respect for others.

CHAPTER 9

48

Factors Contributing To Children And Teens Anxiety

When it comes to teens, it's quite difficult to tell whether their outbursts of displeasure or grief are representative of the current debate over adolescent depression's rights. It is natural for most teenagers to feel unhappy at times.

When the effect of hormones, which are characteristic of that period, is amplified and the diversity of changes that adolescents undergo, it's not difficult to notice that their moods fluctuate from minute to minute.

Nonetheless, evidence indicates that every eighth adolescent suffers from teenage depression. Do not be alarmed, as this type of depression is typically transient and fleeting. However, if this scenario persists for more than two weeks, it will almost probably require the assistance of expert health personnel.

There are several reasons why an adolescent may be depressed or dissatisfied. Due to their low grades in school and the pressure from teachers, teenagers may begin to feel useless and thus lose their previously acquired self-confidence.

Depression can affect poor peer relationships and sexual orientation and the pressures inside the family as an environment that imposes particular values and habits. Also, in some situations, adolescent depression might be triggered by the stress associated with the environment in which each teenager lives.

Regardless of the source of depression, if friends or family are unable to help a teenager overcome it and despite the support of so many, the teenager continues to feel alienated and miserable - this is referred to as an adolescent depression.

The most prevalent symptoms of adolescent depression are that children who are predisposed to this type of depression exhibit noticeable changes in their behavior, thinking, and emotions. As manifested by a teenager, they just lose drive and interest in everything and withdraw.

Also, these children are prone to excessive behavior, insufficient or excessive sleep, dietary alterations and even criminal activity.

Adolescent depression symptoms include the following:

- Apathy headaches and weariness
- Often occurring trouble concentrating
- Difficult decisions
- Extreme guilt is an indication of irresponsible activity
- Failure to meet promises and commitments
- Running away from school
- Short-term memory impairment
- Fixation with death and dying
- Outbursts of despair and distress
- Insomnia
- Alcohol and illicit substances
- Alienation from friends

If your teen exhibits any of aforementioned signs, intervene early to prevent further depression development and assist your youngster in participating in this potentially difficult phase.

Many strategies include conducting more regular and in-depth conversations with children, engaging in objective problem solving, often mixing with children, fostering hobbies, sports and extracurricular activities.

To assist your child in conquering anxiety and panic attacks, put an end to crippling phobias, and regain self-confidence, as a parent, your first step should be to recognize the symptoms afflicting your child's young life.

When parents fail to detect their children's anxiety symptoms, the youngsters typically face unwarranted worries at school and in social situations, resulting in medical ailments and sadness.

Having to face these worries alone, often to the point of being unable to enjoy the simple pleasure of being oneself, many youngsters will carry their issues into their teens and adulthood.

According to current studies, up to one in ten children will develop an anxiety disorder during their formative years. With this in mind, parents need to realize that regardless of the reason for their child's anxiety, the disease is rarely a reflection of their parenting.

Anxiety doesn't need to be a chronic disorder that your child will carry into adulthood. If the child's symptoms are diagnosed, there are programs available that will put an end to your child's suffering within weeks (without resorting to medication or lengthy therapy).

CHAPTER 10

Is Your Teen Suffering from School Anxiety?

Anxiety is a pervasive reality and it is not limited to adults in stressful job environments. In reality, it occurs to youngsters in school as well. The surroundings, the people at school and even parents themselves can all contribute to our children's anxiety, making them feel bad about themselves.

With that said, it's self-evident that we need to address their anxiety issues - and medical intervention is most definitely not the answer. There are many natural anxiety therapies and approaches available to assist our children in overcoming their school-related fears, whether they be social phobias, exams or performance anxieties.

To begin, let us examine the external elements that can contribute to children's worry and the natural anxiety alleviation options that are available:

Parents often assume that most of their expectations are reasonable. They feel their children are brilliant and hence want and expect them to maximize their abilities. What most parents fail to recognize, however, is that living up to their expectations also requires emotional maturity. Intelligent children do not necessarily grow up to be structured, disciplined and driven adults.

Thus, intelligent children may find different situations frustrating, particularly if their parents expect too much of them. What is occasionally wrong with parents is that they push their children too hard or too quickly, detrimental to their growth. Children develop at their pace, so try to be as age-appropriate as possible when setting expectations for your children.

Children and adolescents have a strong tendency to compare themselves to their peers. Children might make intellectual and social comparisons with their peers. Excessive comparison can result in uneasiness. The most effective strategy for combating this and naturally relieving anxiety is to promote positive self-talk.

Teach your children to be encouraging to one another anytime they experience failure or make a mistake. As a parent, you should also engage in positive self-talk. Never pass judgment on someone overtly, as this can only result in irritation, depression and increased anxiety.

Children, too, have emotions. Regrettably, most people do not understand these interior feelings, particularly negative ones such as grief, disappointment and fear. They often end up concealing or burying these emotions.

These suppressed feelings are more likely to return as anxiety or despair over time. By sharing these negative emotions with your children, you may teach them the value of self-awareness.

Teach children to recognize these feelings and to express them in healthy ways. The more positive outlets for children's emotions (through writing, speaking and painting, for example), the less likely they are to harbor negative emotions.

While we as parents tend to take matters into our own hands, this can exacerbate our children's anxiousness. If you believe your child is in an anxiety-inducing scenario, let him work things out on his own first however, if you believe that things will cross the line, which is the time to intercede.

Teaching them self-esteem and self-awareness and decreasing your expectations are all effective approaches to assist your children in overcoming anxiety. Of course, don't forget to inform them that you're also available to assist them.

Social anxiety in children, also known as Social Anxiety Disorder (SAD), is a condition in which your child has difficulties with performance and social situations. This can create difficulties at school and interfere with your child's education, in addition to creating difficulties at home. The following situations are often associated with severe anxiety and fear:

- Beginning a conversation
- Activities with peers that are not structured
- Performing in public
- Taking the initiative in class
- Inviting others to participate or gather

Avoiding these activities may have a detrimental effect on the child's intellectual advancement and capacity to have and make friends with peers their age.

Social Anxiety typically strikes youngsters throughout their tween/teen adolescent years, when friendships and social activities are important for mature growth. It is worthwhile to get professional care for a child who suffers from Social Anxiety Disorder. It impairs healthy social and emotional development and increases the risk of depression and substance usage.

You cannot always rely on teachers to notify you or refer your child for help, as they may dismiss it as shyness or conclude that it is not a problem because it is not disruptive.

Social Anxiety Disorder Symptoms

The following are some indicators of Social Anxiety in children:

- Hesitates and avoids being the center of attention
- Avoidance or refusal to begin conversations, perform in public, invite friends to meet, contact others for homework or other information or order food at restaurants
- Attempting to avoid eye contact
- Very softly spoken or mumbled
- Peer engagement and discourse are minimal.
- Appearing solitary or on the group's periphery
- Sitting alone at the library or café or keeping a safe distance from a group of people during team meetings
- Concerned excessively with negative assessment, shame or embarrassment

- Difficulty communicating in public, reading aloud or being called upon in class

Now, keep in mind that all children experience these issues at some point and that some children are just naturally shy. I remember being so timid in school that I would break out in a cold sweat if required to speak in front of the class.

Consider all these indicators in combination; if they persist for an extended length of time and are causing problems for your kid, it is time to consult your primary care physician. When children are placed in these types of situations, the following physical indications indicate Social Anxiety:

- Sweating
- Heart pounding
- Stomachache
- Dizziness
- Tantrums of Weeping

As I previously stated, these are indicators in a youngster that may indicate a social anxiety disorder. Of course, some children will utilize these tools to avoid doing their schoolwork! That is one of the reasons symptoms must remain for an extended period, at least a month.

If your child avoids social situations, struggles in school or is fully withdrawn at home, please document your observations and schedule an appointment with your child's doctor.

Bring your list of observations to your doctor's appointment to demonstrate what occurred, when, where and the frequency of occurrence. Your doctor will also assist you in determining whether there is a problem or refer you to a specialist in Social Anxiety in Children.

CHAPTER 11

Depression in Adolescents: They Refuse to Be Things

Teen depression is on the rise and appears to be on the verge of continuing to rise. According to Mental Health America, the suicide rate among teenagers and young adults has nearly tripled since 1960. When it comes to adolescent depression, this statistic now includes girls between the ages of 12 and 17.

Adults' mental health is becoming a concern as well. Psychotropic drug use is soaring.

Do we require more effective medications?

Do we have to incorporate medications into our regular diet?

Many teenagers, understandably, do not want to be a part of such an inhumane way of life. The solution, however, is not suicide; rather, it is about raising consciousness and reconstructing a more human society.

A more human society

A more humane society respects human nature and this is where we get into trouble.

What is favorable to human nature and what is antagonistic to it?

This is difficult to explain since concepts about human nature have been established to justify various systems of social structure throughout human history. Many avenues exist for us to begin our inquiry of human nature. However, my preferred way is self-observation.

Although we might conceive many alternative methods for doing such an analysis, I grew to be wary of any explanation of human nature provided by individuals who:

* Desire for you to accept their definition without allowing you to verify its integrity independently

* Have a selfish interest in your acceptance of this definition

* Hold positions of power and may lose them if you do not subscribe to their way of thinking

Unfortunately, we must be tenacious in our hunt for an unbiased source of human nature. Many biased sources will obstruct your efforts and the good ones are scarce.

My interpretation of actual human nature

I'd want to share with you my idea of actual human nature. I've been working on it for some years, persuaded that true change would occur only when each of us begins to recognize the truth about human nature for ourselves, rather than depending on established learned definitions.

Children, paradoxically, are among the best teachers of human nature, owing to their objectivity.

Depression in adolescents, in my opinion, results from a struggle between the unbiased human nature of teenagers and the external pressure placed on them to conform to the sick and artificial form of human nature that society proposes.

Man in the modern era is a thing.

Modern man is, in some ways, more of a thing than a true human being. He self-sells. He polishes himself in the same manner that apples are polished to entice consumers. He spends years studying, learning languages and polishing his manners to improve his value and sell himself at a greater price, just like the apples do.

The market establishes his market worth. If the market prefers extroverts, he will become one. If introverts are revalued, they will become one. If the market desires happy individuals, he will grin even if he is in agony on the inside.

Considerable effort is expended in determining what sells on the market and the apple, er, the human being, is polished accordingly. Any market movement can cause your value to vanish quickly. This contributes to feelings of insecurity and worry.

Teenagers that are depressed do not wish to be things.

Depressed adolescents intuitively refuse to view themselves as consumable objects. If they had the freedom to articulate this opposition, they would ask, "What is the sense of existing if I have to become a consumable object?"

I propose that we allow children to express this refusal intentionally and learn how to make our society more human.

CHAPTER 12

61

What Are the Distinctions Between Anxiety and Depression in Children and Teenagers

Around half of the children who suffer from depression also suffer from anxiety. Anxiety is easy to miss since a youngster, particularly a teenager, may not express his anxieties. Young children are far more receptive and comfortable discussing their anxieties and concerns.

Anxiety typically manifests itself in one of two ways:

1. A disorder of widespread anxiety

2. Panic attack-related anxiety.

Generalized anxiety symptoms include restlessness, a sense of being on edge, being overwhelmed, difficulty concentrating and muscle tightness or sleep problems. There may be more anxieties with generalized anxiety but they are not as strong as during a panic attack.

The most prevalent panic attacks in children are school phobia and separation anxiety, which occurs when a youngster must leave the physical closeness. Children who are normally well behaved may become so frightened in some situations that they vomit, have severe temper tantrums and act defiantly.

Anxiety is distinct from depression in that an anxious youngster typically has more energy and a less pessimistic outlook on life. Other than that, the anxious youngster is fearful and experiences worries that impair his capacity to meet the obligations imposed upon him. Anxiety can impair his ability to attend school, participate in social activities and just relax.

While the anxious youngster may avoid activities, he does it differently than the depressed child. The anxious child will attempt to avoid circumstances that make him apprehensive.

The sad youngster avoids confronting a situation because he lacks the energy and tolerance for irritation necessary to do so. Also, the nervous youngster feels the stress of perceived bad occurrences more acutely.

However, anxiety and depression have one feature. Threats about the negative repercussions of a child's behavior nearly never work. Other than that, they are likely to exacerbate the situation.

Threatening an anxious child will only serve to increase his or her worry and trigger an "Oh, on!" response. The depressed youngster may be unable to respond to the threat due to a lack of energy or motivation, resulting in a "So what?" response.

Understanding the reasons for a child's depression might assist parents in recognizing it. On the other side, if a youngster suffering from anxiety and depression understands what he is going through, it can

help him recognize that he cannot allow his past to ruin his future and motivate him to overcome his anxiety and despair.

Causes:

1) Child Abuse

Child abuse is so prevalent in our horrible world filled with violence and selfishness. The defenseless infant is just too young to face such trauma. Child abuse victims suffer physical, emotional, mental, moral and even spiritual harm. As individuals age, all these painful memories from their childhood begin to dominate their life visions.

Most of them will engage in violent behavior and abuse drugs and alcohol. The anguish and disappointments etched into their brains and emotions will lead them to believe that their lives are nothing more than a jumble of grief and pain. They believe they are strong, yet they are quite frail. They are not afraid to fight and injure others but they prefer solitude and even wish to die.

2) A family in disarray

Children of divorced couples are emotionally devastated from an early age of confusion and loss. Children require both parents' love and attention. When this natural emotional yearning is not satisfied, things seem so unfair. They develop a sense of doubt, insecurity and rebelliousness as they mature.

3) Injustice treatment or upbringing in a family devoid of love

In some families, parents prioritize one child over the other. This often results in feelings of envy and jealousy. Our children crave attention and they get quickly envious when we lavish attention on others. They feel abandoned and insecure and often believe they are no longer loved.

Failure to show children fair love and care can crush their hearts and cause them to treat others with hatred, just as they were treated previously. It's simple to distinguish between a youngster reared with affection and one raised with harshness and harsh treatment.

The latter is often more disobedient and troublemaker. This will develop a sense of guilt and irritation, which will eventually transform into unhappiness and worry.

4) Inheritance

This has something to do with genetic mental illness. Children of mentally ill parents often behave similarly. They will experience loneliness and depression for no apparent reason.

These are few of the reasons why children and adolescents become depressed. We must then demonstrate our love and care for them and assist them in coping with their circumstances. They are too young to endure all of life's miseries and if left addressed, will wreak havoc on their entire lives.

Do not despair if your child's situation appears hopeless. There are helpful strategies for assisting him in coping with this.

CHAPTER 13

65

What Teachers and Parents Need to Know About Adolescent and Young Adult Suicide

Suicide is one of the leading causes of death in adolescents. The latest mean annual suicide rates per 100,000 people globally are 0.5 for females and 0.9 for males between the ages of 5 and 14 and 12.0 for females and 14.2 for males between 15 and 24.

Males outnumber females in most nations when it comes to teenage suicide statistics. Suicidal attempts and gestures are significantly more often than completed suicides. According to one epidemiological study, for every completed suicide, there were approximately 23 suicidal gestures and attempts.

While female adolescents are significantly more likely to attempt suicide than male adolescents, male adolescents are more likely to commit suicide. In the previous three decades, the suicide rate among young adolescents and young adults has climbed by more than 300 percent.

SUICIDE RISK FACTORS

Contrary to common opinion, suicide is not an impulsive act but the consequence of a three-step process: a prior history of issues is reinforced by adolescent troubles; lastly, a triggering event, either a death or the end of a major relationship, causes the suicide.

The key risk factors for suicide among adolescents that have been scientifically established are listed below.

DESCRIPTIONS OF PERSONAL CHARACTERISTICS

Psychopathology: Over 90% of juvenile suicide victims and over 60% of younger adolescent suicide victims have at least one significant psychiatric illness. Depressive disorders are the most prevalent disorder among adolescent suicide victims.

Depression that appears to resolve spontaneously is cause for caution and the early stages of recovery from depression might be hazardous. Other disorders shown to be prevalent in this demographic include substance misuse, behavior disorder, posttraumatic stress disorder and panic attacks.

Suicide has been connected to cognitive and psychological variables such as hopelessness, impaired interpersonal problem-solving abilities and aggressive impulsive behavior.

Biological factors: Some teenagers are predisposed to suicide due to their physiological constitution. Serotonin dysfunction, a neurotransmitter, has been linked to suicidal behavior.

THE FAMILY CHARACTERISTICS

Suicidal behavior in the family: Teens who commit suicide often had a close family member who attempted or committed suicide.

High rates of parental psychopathology, particularly depression and substance misuse, have been linked to completed suicide and suicidal ideation and attempts in teenagers. Also, family connectedness is protective against suicide behavior in teenagers.

ADVERSE LIFE SITUATIONS

Stressful life events: In adolescents, life stressors such as interpersonal losses and legal or disciplinary problems are connected with attempted suicide and completed suicide. Also, the anniversary of a loss can elicit a strong desire to commit suicide.

Physical abuse in childhood has been linked to an increased incidence of suicide attempts during late adolescence and early adulthood.

SOCIOECONOMIC AND CONTEXTUAL DEVELOPMENT FACTORS

Education and job problems: Difficulties in school, inability to work or attend school, dropping out of high school and not enrolling in college all increase the chance of committing suicide.

Teens are more likely to try suicide if they have recently read, seen or heard about another teen's suicide attempt. Suicide cluster studies and the media's impact continue to accumulate evidence confirming the reality of suicide contagion. Suicide stories appear to have the biggest effect on subsequently attempted suicides among youths.

CHAPTER 14

69

How to Detect Teen Substance Abuse

Nothing is more detrimental to a teen's development and/or family than drug usage. As a result, the earlier intervention can be carried out, the better. In most cases, the issue is that kids use narcotics for many months, if not years before their parents become aware. Even when parents become aware of their child's drug usage, they often underestimate its extent.

Signs of Substance Abuse

Do not ignore the warning signs if you suspect your child is misusing drugs. Addiction is tough for children to understand. All of us believe that we can handle any form of danger, no matter how big or small. As a result of the constant pressures of adolescence, some teenagers turn to drugs as a means of escaping the realities of their lives.

- Disregard for appearance/hygiene
- Self-esteem issues
- Grades are slipping
- At-home violent outbursts
- Frequent use of eyewash
- Unexplained weight loss
- Paraphernalia for narcotics consumption
- Slurred Speech
- Taking flight
- Skin Abrasions
- Breath of chemicals
- Glacial eyes
- Valuables have gone missing
- Intolerance of family members
- Red eyes
- Money theft/borrowing
- Unexpectedly, valuables materialize in the child's possession.

- Friendships change
- Depression
- Withdrawal
- Apathy
- Imprudent Behavior
- There is no concern for the future.
- Defies Values of the Family
- Parents are treated with contempt
- Lying/deceptive
- Suspicious conduct
- Ignores the repercussions
- Loss of interest in physically active pursuits
- Abusive verbally
- Manipulative/self-centered
- Inadequate motivation
- Truancy

If your child's conduct exhibits any of these warning signs, a harmful pattern may be developing that necessitates action

A denial or shame-based attitude to drug abuse will only add to the difficulty of overcoming it. If action is necessary, effective assistance is available. By calling 1-800-637-0701, Teen Help can connect you with effective options.

Conscientious Parenting

Parents often express a desire to know all that is happening in their children's life. However, is this truly true? Parents should understand that drug use typically begins months, if not years before parents become aware of their teen's use.

Some problems, such as children's sexual activity, underage drinking and gang violence, are so upsetting that parents often prefer to ignore them or address them only lightly, often wrapped in denial and believing these concerns will not touch their family. Parents are aware that the ramifications of these difficulties can be terrifying, if not fatal.

However, silently clinging to denial and the hope that these concerns will not affect their children's lives can have a similarly terrible effect. No subject is more terrifying to a parent than adolescent substance misuse.

Parenting poses ongoing difficulties. Placing blinders on will never result in resolutions. The subject of adolescent drug misuse is vast and varied, encompassing different drugs and their variants.

Although we cannot cover all aspects of drug misuse among adolescents in this article, our goal is to offer you a better understanding so that you can make better judgments regarding your children's adolescent drug use.

Why do children experiment with drugs?

While we seek methods to safeguard our children from the dangers of substance misuse, the question of why they would ever desire to use them arises. Adults often ask, "Who is to blame?" Adults are often seeking to deflect responsibility and often point the finger of blame outward.

If you ask around, you may hear a variety of concerns, ranging from the media to peer influence to poor school supervision to the lack of authority of drug pushers and law enforcement to the overreaction of law enforcement to the lack of involvement of parents.

There is no doubting that these elements can play a role, as external effects can be rather potent. However, blaming external factors alone would be an exaggeration, as it would imply that our children are merely victims of circumstance, absolving them of responsibility for their own choices.

Whereas adults often look externally for "the answers," children's explanations often point inward. They often justify it more personally, as if something within them is pulling them on; a need to fit in, a curiosity or a want for the thrill. Understanding the teen perspective is important.

When asked why their comments include the following:

- They desire to fit in, to have a sense of belonging.
- To rebel against adult authority to find an escape route from their issues
- To conceal their incompetence and low self-esteem
- The thrill and exhilaration of taking a chance
- Desiring to feel mature

The "Gateway" Substances

Most adolescents do not start with so-called "hard drugs" like cocaine, crystal meth or heroin. Usage typically begins with significantly more readily available and legal substances in the adult population: nicotine and alcohol. Usage typically begins with ready access to these items in a person's home, whether their own, friends, or relatives.

Many specialists often think tobacco and alcohol are the "gateway" or "entry" to a road into drug dependence. Even adolescents are generally aware of the substantial health dangers linked with smoking. However, if they are willing to smoke, the relationship to drinking alcohol is obvious.

By this point, they have established themselves as risk-takers and the logical next step is to marijuana. From there, it's possible to slide dangerously, even fatally, towards other drugs and the destructive habits that accompany them.

Recognize Addictive Behavior

Regardless of the drug, the disease of addiction appears to have a predictable path. Generally, the user begins out of curiosity. If the initial experience is pleasurable, the user is more than likely to continue using the substance recreationally, such as with friends, at parties or on weekends.

As they grow to like the drug more and more, their consumption would inevitably escalate to the point where they regularly use it during the week.

Eventually, their lives become increasingly oriented on obtaining the drug and locating occasions to take it. It begins to disrupt their relationships, school, employment and other previously productive areas of their lives.

Drug dependence or addiction has taken hold and the individual is incapable of functioning without the substance. If there is no physical dependence on their substance of choice, there is almost certainly a psychological dependence. If their preferred medication is not readily available, they will go to any length to obtain it.

What You Need to Know About Marijuana

Tobacco, as measured by the National Institute on Drug Abuse, is the most commonly used illegal substance in the United States today. About half of all high school students had tried marijuana at some time in their lives, according to the data.

Many teenagers dabbled with marijuana during their college years and now find it difficult to discuss marijuana use with their children. However, marijuana usage has begun at a much younger age in the modern era and children now have access to a much more potent type of marijuana.

Children describe their marijuana usage as a way to cope with life's difficulties, to cope with worry, rage or depression, as a way to escape, as something to do to alleviate boredom. Long-term studies of high school students indicate that few young people experiment with other substances without first using marijuana. Marijuanais a gateway drug, in and of itself.

Huffing - The Silent Epidemic

The National Institute on Drug Abuse reports that over 1,000 commonly used household and classroom goods can be used as inhalants. "Huffing" is a sort of drug misuse that is rapidly gaining popularity among our youth. Because these things are so prevalent, you are unlikely to be alarmed if you see an adolescent purchasing them.

After all, would you believe that anything as innocuous as whipped cream, hair spray, or air freshener could be abused as a dangerous drug? These goods often contain butane or toluene, which are corrosive to the kidneys, liver and bone marrow and can even induce brain damage.

CHAPTER 15

76

How to Deal With a Depressed Child

Depression in adolescents and teenagers is just as common as it is in adults, and as such, it must be taken seriously and addressed.

The earlier parents are alerted to their children's depressive symptoms, the better equipped they are to deal with it. If you don't do anything about it, depression will return. First, you need to know what to watch for in your child's behavior, so be on the lookout for any indicators.

Consider these signs if you're worried about the well-being of your child or adolescent:

- Decreased or increased hunger, restlessness, or daytime sleepiness are all symptoms of sleep disturbances.
- Lonely teen, child not playing
- Low self-esteem, negative self-criticism - Feels enraged and/or bored
- Discusses death (says things like "I wish I had never been born/was dead")
- Friendships and parent-child relationships have changed as a result of this (friends and parent-child relationships)
- Crying and outbursts
- Anxiety, acute fears, paranoia

Please remember that a depressive youngster or adolescent is unlikely to express himself as sad or depressed but rather as bored, angry or unhappy.

Of course, some of these symptoms may occur in the absence of depression and may simply be a natural response to something upsetting. That is why you must ascertain its duration. If the episode lasts more than two weeks, it is more likely to be a depressive episode.

Your attitude and behavior toward your sad child are important—also, your comprehension. Indeed, you must assess his school and home surroundings to determine what precipitated his depression. Family conflicts can significantly influence children who may feel guilty or rejected. Therefore, if you are aware of the cause and can effect change, take action.

Now, here are some suggestions for assisting your melancholy child:

Assure him of your concern for his despair. Assure him that he is neither insane nor odd. It is natural to feel melancholy when confronted with a difficult scenario. It's only that some people have an illness that makes recovery from such melancholy more difficult. Allow him to have these feelings or he will conceal them.

Always keep in mind how he views things and how something as seemingly unimportant to you as the loss of a pet or a remark from a friend may be to him. Be patient with him and never downplay what he is going through, as an example.

Always tell the truth. Hiding it does nothing to safeguard your child and help him feel trustworthy and capable of overcoming obstacles with your assistance.

Discuss depression with your child, how it works, how he feels and why. Indicate who he may speak with (you, a favorite uncle, teacher, etc.)

There are several ways to obtain aid, from a professional to a parenting method. I don't think it's a good idea to put your depressed child on medication. According to the FDA, antidepressant medications can increase the risk of suicidal behavior in children and adolescents.

However, I can offer you some advice on parenting techniques you may wish to employ. Indeed, some parenting programs have been developed to help parents improve their relationships with their children and assist them in living happy and healthy lives.

They provide effective and simple-to-implement advice and communication tools to assist you in resolving any issues your child or you may be experiencing, such as depression.

CHAPTER 16

Parenting Troubled Adolescents

Parenting disturbed adolescents presents a significant challenge for many parents. Troubled teens are young adults who have experienced or are now experiencing alcohol or drug misuse, depression, attention deficit disorder, disrespect or a negative attitude.

They often fail to achieve their life goals and may have a negative influence on others. A good parent will never allow their children to endanger their own or others' lives.

Teenage is often the most trying time in a child's life. Throughout the adolescent years, a child's emotions, hormone levels and worldview evolve. Also, adolescence is a stressful time for children. Like adults, children and adolescents respond to stress differently, including withdrawal, getting angry or sad or becoming a drug addict.

Troubled children often have a sense of alienation from their families, which indicates previous familial dysfunction. Teen parenthood is often motivated by a desire to develop a deep bond with the children. Even if you lament your child's upbringing, building a good bond is not too late. With a younger child, it is very easy to develop a strong attachment.

Develop a relationship with your teen through his interests. This does not imply that he may leave whenever he pleases.

Other than that, you must find a method to involve him in activities that he enjoys. For instance, take your child to a video game store, allow him to select his favorite game and take it home with you to play. As a result, parents can easily connect with their teenagers through objects, thoughts and experiences that uplift and energize their spirit.

When you discover that you have lost contact with your child, consult a psychiatrist to determine the best method of communication. The new approach must be sincere and focused on your affection for him and your concern for his future and safety.

Signs of Imminence

As parents of teenagers, we often overlook the warning signals of a disturbed adolescent. This indicates that your adolescent is exhibiting some bad behaviors in an attempt to gain your attention.

However, due to your difficulties, you may be blind to your child's. We are all busy with our own lives, but as parents, we are responsible for staying informed about our children's lives and guiding them toward fruitful adulthood.

Even though your youngster is seventeen and on the verge of emancipation, he or she continues to think like a child, not an adult. Isolation, a new group of friends, academic difficulties, drug and alcohol usage and melancholy or anxiety are warning indicators of a problematic teen.

Isolation of Your Adolescent

For your adolescent, having friends means the world. If you see that your teen is spending an increasing amount of time alone, it's time to figure out why. While some teenagers are extremely timid, they all have at least one best friend.

Peer Groups

New acquaintances you've never met - this indicates DANGER. If your adolescent begins hanging out with an entirely new set of pals and never mentions their identities or where they live, it's time to coax the information out of her.

You're probably familiar with the adage, "One bad apple ruins the whole lot." You surely do not want one terrible adolescent to spoil your child. Your teen may also begin dressing differently to fit in with her new friends. This is yet another cue for you to enter.

Issues at School

Falling grades or lying about not finishing assignments are indicators that your teen's behavior has shifted. If she consistently fails to complete assignments even though you have asked her if she did her work and has always responded "yes," then something is amiss and it's time to figure out what is wrong.

At times, a teenager will simply refuse to attend school and her absenteeism will skyrocket. Your adolescent may develop conflicts with some of their teachers. These are all red flags that you should intervene and assist your kid to the best of your ability or seek professional help for her.

Alcohol and Drugs

Trying a little booze or dabbling with pot may be a normal part of the adolescent experience in this day and age. However, something has changed when a parent's medicines go missing or your child exhibits unpredictable and weird behavior. When in doubt, verify.

While some may take a strong stance against the following advice, it may save your child's life. When your teenager leaves for school, check through her room, paying close attention to the back of her dresser drawers.

You may discover that your child does indeed have some serious mental problems, particularly if the term "suicide" appears in your computer's search engine. Also, your teen may begin wearing long-sleeved clothes to protect herself from razor blade cuts.

These are all indicators that you, as a parent, must intervene and give assistance. You do not want your adolescent to commit the unthinkable.

Here's another warning sign: if your youngster vanishes immediately after eating or eats very little, do not allow this to continue. Our daughter was diagnosed with anorexia nervosa and bulimia. We could have detected it sooner but our eyes were opened when she began passing out. This can occur in both boys and girls.

Children are a gift from God, therefore treat them with respect. Paying attention to your children is the most crucial piece of advise

I can give you. Acquaint yourself with them, their likes and dislikes, habits, wardrobe and social circle. If you are actively involved, you will identify early warning signs of trouble and intervene to assist.

Our most serious public health concern is the isolation and loss of our children.

The latest YouTube video of a teen committing suicide in front of millions of viewers should serve as a frightening warning to all parents. Our children are paying a high price as families face increasing financial, emotional and physical strain.

What does it take to get the parent's attention?

When my son Jason was about fifteen years old, the teenage son of a friend committed suicide. The boy's girlfriend and the type of music she urged him to listen to were identified as a possible reason. She was eventually found guilty and charged with being an accomplice to murder in a civil trial.

Today's children have more dramatic methods of suicide. Still, this episode shocked me into going through all of my son's music, interrogating him about some of the bands he listened to and becoming more acutely aware of his whereabouts. My attention was drawn to the image of a toddler hanging himself. As more youngsters "reach out" in inappropriate ways to be heard, parents must prioritize their children's needs.

As a mental health specialist, I witness the desperation of teenagers attempting to fit into an increasingly demanding society, striving to feel good about themselves and seeking methods to meet their basic needs.

Everyone recognizes that the adolescent years are some of the most trying for everyone. Yet, we sometimes believe that teenagers should be able to care for themselves, handle their daily routines independently and be essentially "grown-up." Nothing could be more erroneous! I educate parents about their children's three important developmental stages. Two of them may astound you.

The first stage is known as the dreadful or fantastic two's, depending on how parents perceive it if you view this stage as a chance to assist your children in developing a strong sense of independence and owning their power.

You will view "no!" and "I can do it myself!" as necessary steps in the process and will promote independence rather than punish it. It is a significant chance to assist children in determining their identity in connection to their world and in developing self-esteem. How we treat the years two to four is essential for our children.

The twelve to fourteen-year-old is the next stage. I tell parents that this time is similar to being two years old, except they are both bigger and smarter. Prepare yourself! Again, your youngster requires significant encouragement and assistance.

They will simultaneously push you away and pull you in, much as a two-year-old does. I believe the requirements are nearly identical but the appearance is different.

I recall my kid informing me "Please, mom, do not attempt to kiss me goodbye when you drop me off for football practice! Everybody will notice you!" Everything is important for this age group in terms of how their peers perceive them. With a two-year-old, it's all about how you perceive them. Both are occasions to exercise patience and maintain a kind and continuous presence in their face.

The third opportunity for intense parenting occurs between the ages of eighteen and twenty. Children are going through an identity crisis, regardless of whether you believe it or not. Every stage of emotional growth necessitates your assistance, so please be there to lend a hand.

How many couples do you know who waited till the children left to end their unsuccessful marriages?

It is one of the most trying periods you can imagine for your children. The family structure contributes to the ease with which children transition to adulthood. Suppose you have to leave, the sooner the better. Divorce is difficult for all children but older children suffer the most. I am not recommending that you stay for the sake of your children.

That is never in their best interests, in my opinion. At any age, the damage divorce does to children is more a function of how the parents handle the divorce process and their joint parenting role than of the divorce itself.

Here are some pointers for navigating these difficult times:

Begin by paying close attention to each important stage. Ensure that you conduct a mental health check on every member of the family.

Take charge of your tension and anger. Recognize the impact of anxiety, depression and other emotional difficulties on your children.

Communication is your most significant tool when it comes to your children. If it is shattered, the connection is shattered. Peers will begin to take precedence over you. Allow this not to happen. If your communication begins to deteriorate, seek assistance.

Develop your listening and patience skills.

Establish unambiguous boundaries and expectations. Check these out with your older children to ensure they are included in the decision-making process on rules and expectations. Begin by providing options for your two-year-old.

Inquire often. At all ages, questions motivate students to solve their problems WITH YOUR HELP. This helps to develop internal discipline. Above all, parents from a place of love, not fear.

CHAPTER 17

Children's Emotional Resilience

Emotional resilience is the capacity to cope effectively and meaningfully with stressful life experiences, disappointments and challenges, preserve self-esteem, develop social aptitude and avoid frustration, rage and even depression. Emotional resilience developed early in life assists in the recovery process following setbacks and disappointments, promoting emotional wellness.

Teach your child to be emotionally resilient and he or she will get the control and confidence necessary to deal through difficult situations effectively. Developing emotional resilience during childhood lays the groundwork for your child's emotional wellness throughout adolescence and adulthood.

Emotions influence how your child interacts with others and the behaviors that result from those encounters. To avoid conflict or to cope with it effectively when it occurs, your child should develop an understanding of his or her feelings, the ability to identify and control them.

It is important to teach youngsters that different emotions can be expressed in different ways. However, understanding how to communicate them effectively will aid your youngster in resolving social disputes and preserving connections.

One strategy to foster emotional competence is to assist your child in developing a vocabulary for expressing emotions. Also, parents can educate their children in detecting distinct emotions and educating them that their thoughts can change their emotions.

Actions trigger emotions. However, youngsters must learn that their emotions should not dictate their behavior. Youngsters need to understand that expressing their emotions assists in the prevention and resolution of problems. They must learn that suppressed emotions result in misunderstandings, worry, rage and sadness.

When your child cannot communicate his or her feelings, he or she is more likely to encounter furious outbursts caused by sadness, embarrassment or frustration.

Perhaps your child feels guilty about something he or she has done, is terrified or feels helpless and chooses to vent these negative emotions of emotional tension through furious outbursts. This failure to deal constructively with stress is often the result of a lack of knowledge of one's own emotions, the emotions, and the inability to articulate sentiments properly.

Emotional Fragility Symptoms
- Withdrawal
- Behavior regression
- Bedwetting - Nightmares
- Excessive clinginess

Promoting positive family communication is one of the most important things a parent can encourage healthy emotional development. This involves positive reinforcement, which involves praising your child for appropriate behaviors, encouraging them and refraining from negative criticism when expected outcomes are not met.

Also, consistency is important for a child's mental health since it helps eliminate ambiguity and uncertainty. When youngsters understand what is expected of them, they are more likely to cooperate, avoiding irritation, rage and potential embarrassment.

Younger children may be more receptive and willing to communicate their emotions. Family communication may become more difficult during adolescence as the teen attempts to suppress their sentiments to address them independently.

Sustaining a relationship with a teenager demands patience and the capacity to be supportive. Frequently, conversing with your teen at home might be difficult.

However, your teen may attempt to open up while traveling in a car with you without making eye contact, making the confrontation appear less daunting. Establishing a strong emotional resilience foundation in childhood will aid your adolescent in achieving emotional health.

If communicating with your child becomes difficult or if he or she withdraws and displays signs of emotional instability, do not hesitate to seek help. Consult another family member, a friend or a counselor to begin.

CHAPTER 18

91

Make an Alert for a Depressed Teen

Depression does not just affect adults; it is one of the most prevalent mental health diseases among adolescents in affluent countries. Every fifth adolescent has depressive moods and feelings, although depression in teenagers is often misdiagnosed professionally.

A depressed teen might develop for different reasons and their moods often fluctuate, from mild depression to overpowering melancholy that is quite worrying. Depression has developed into a global disease afflicting people of all ages, sexes and socioeconomic positions.

Teen depression is a serious problem and the gloomy numbers underscore the urgency with which the issue must be tackled promptly.

Seasonal depression affects a small percentage of teenagers but 5% of adolescents suffer from serious depression. If no action is taken, further mental problems such as antisocial conduct, drug or alcohol addiction and juvenile delinquency might emerge from early depressions.

Because depression is a hereditary disorder, inheritance is considered a substantial risk factor.

Substance misuse can affect up to a third of youth who are depressed.

Depression or another psychological disease predates and plays a significant role in the overwhelming majority of suicide youths. Bipolar disorder, a more serious mental illness than depression, often develops in untreated youth for despair.

Teen depression can be transient or chronic. Occasional breakouts of teen depression require the attention and aid of those who have direct contact with a teen to avert the unfortunate development.

If left unnoticed and unassisted, the occasional form can develop into a chronic, severe type that requires immediate care by a mental health specialist and can have grave effects if left untreated. Teachers and parents are responsible for monitoring their adolescents and intervening as early as possible to avert a disastrous detour.

Symptoms of teenage depression

Observe your adolescent to identify early indications of depression! Make a note if any of those symptoms are present!

- Chronically low mood that lasts most of the day on most days
- This can be demonstrated via irritability rather than depression.
- Appetite problems or overeating]
- Sleep apnea or hypersomnia
- Low energy or exhaustion
- Low Self-esteem
- Inability to concentrate or make decisions
- Hopelessness
- Low levels of interest and dwindling social contacts.
- Self-criticism, based on uninteresting, incompetent or ineffectual self-concepts

Many types of substance abuse might become co-occurring problems for a teen who is depressed. Children who perform poorly in school, appear withdrawn, act impulsively or demonstrate a lack of interest in previously loved activities should be screened for depression by experienced professionals to identify a problem as early as feasible.

Many adolescents who experience spells of depression can conceal their symptoms from their immediate environment, including parents, peers and teachers. As part of parenting an adolescent, mental health professionals encourage parents and teachers to be vigilant for indicators of depression in their children.

It is important to understand that kids can be treated for depression with the support of mental health specialists and therapists in most situations, provided the appropriate treatment technique is selected and implemented.

That is why early detection and referral to a specialist are important. As previously said, inheritance of depression is a significant risk factor but social rejection, death, loss of connection, loss of hopes and dreams, abandonment, traumatic incident or failing grades for a youngster can also result in an outpouring of worries progresses to depression.

Depression treatment, which is typically a combination of therapies with the possibility of medication use, should be determined by a skilled practitioner. The appropriate method typically produces the desired results regardless of the method chosen - psychotherapy, cognitive behavioral therapy or interpersonal therapy.

In more complex cases, antidepressant medications are prescribed in addition to treatment sessions. Self-help books can be beneficial in assisting with the treatment of teen depression.

While maintaining social relations with someone depressed can be challenging, it is important not to overlook a young person's sentiments. Knowing that friends, parents and classmates care and are willing to lend help can be an important first step toward recovery from depression.

Sustaining a supportive relationship with your kid and cultivating a caring atmosphere around him is the most effective strategy to encourage and motivate the depressed adolescent on his path to recovery.

It is important to conclude that society is beginning to realize that depressions and depression-like diseases do not manifest themselves abruptly at the age of 18 but often have childhood antecedents.

Early diagnosis and appropriate therapy tailored to a teen's specific needs is the most effective strategy to assist a person in overcoming childhood depressions and raising a joyful, productive new generation.

CHAPTER 19

The Best Strategies for Dealing With Your Troubled Teen, Whether or Not They Have Teenage Alcoholism

Teenagers are notoriously difficult to raise. It is a time when their behavior is impulsive, when they are more prone to take risks and when they are separating from their parents in pursuit of independence. These are trying times for all parents.

A problematic adolescent, on the other hand, tears a family apart. Every member of the family suffers unless the parents employ efficient techniques to enlist the assistance of their teen and themselves to turn things around.

Often, juvenile substance misuse is the urgent issue with which their disturbed adolescent is grappling. Adolescent alcoholism and drug misuse must be addressed first. Adolescent drug and alcohol abuse are just too harmful to ignore. Once the youngster is sober, it is important to assess any underlying concerns that may have contributed to the substance misuse (depression, anxiety etc.).

Consider the following extreme situation:

Y.L. was a sixteen-year-old child in my practice who demonstrated a lack of regard for his parents. He took drugs and alcohol, struggled academically and eventually fled.

Authorities apprehended him in another city after being discovered urinating on a building. His parents enrolled him at an adolescent wilderness camp in another country, where he thrived in a highly controlled setting with rigorous adherence to boundaries.

He developed skills for impulse control in this type of atmosphere, which aided him after the program concluded. Of course, not all teenagers are thus challenging. When he returned, his parents needed to learn the skills I've given below to improve the family's position.

The following are the ten best strategies for dealing with a troubled adolescent, with or without teen substance abuse:

Suppose your kid is exhibiting signs of substance misuse (whether it is teenage drinking or teenage drug abuse). In that case, it is necessary to take him or her to a medical expert knowledgeable about treating addiction (most family physicians and pediatricians are).

Also, a psychiatrist who specializes in addiction would be an excellent alternative). A physician can assist in determining the extent of the abuse and whether detoxification or rehabilitation is necessary.

Unambiguous boundaries must be established. For instance, if your teen has a history of substance abuse and relapses, a clear plan of action must be in place (returning to a 12-step program, taking prescribed medication, etc.). Your teen cannot have a car or a cell phone or go out with friends until he or she has demonstrated that they are on the path to recovery.

Your kid should discuss the consequences of violating curfews, using drugs or alcohol, amassing large texting bills, skipping classes or performing poorly in school. Ascertain that these implications are obvious, whether they include the loss of Internet access, a cell phone or a car.

Be an excellent role model. If you drink and drive, your child is likely to do the same. If you model drinking and verbal abuse for your child, you establish an example for your teen to follow. If you tell your teen a falsehood, he or she will learn to lie. Also, if you are honest and fair with your teen, this will have a beneficial effect.

Participate in your teen's life. Inquire as to your teen's social circle. Understand your teen's interests.

What genres of music is your youngster a fan of?

What are their favorite school subjects? What television shows are they now watching?

Which YouTube videos are their favorites?

Maintain structured activities for your teens, such as athletics and music. Participating in sports or learning to play a musical instrument is beneficial to one's health and self-esteem. Your teen's well-being is at risk if he or she spends too much time unstructured.

As a family, have dinner together. Consumption of food as a family truly results in a decrease in teen substance addiction.

Communicate with your teen openly and calmly. Your teen will shut off if you yell or lecture.

Praise your teen for each improvement he or she achieves. Even if your teen may never confess it, your teen still seeks your approval.

Be a parent to your teen, not a friend. Your teen relies on you to be consistent yet tough to help him or her navigate this period of emotional turmoil.

Early in my psychiatric career, I saw that parents who behaved more like friends to their teens than a parent had the most troublesome children. Your teen requires caring parents who appreciate him or her and are capable of setting proper boundaries.

Maintain your involvement. Keep a close check on your teen's behavior. Addiction is not something that should be disregarded, despite what many believe. Remain open to the possibility of new ideas. Have a good time as a family. Your teen requires you more than ever during this dance of separation.

CHAPTER 20

Treating Your Depressed Adolescent

Depression is one of the most prevalent ailments in the United States today and many physicians like to toss antidepressants about like candy to resolve the issue. This is a significant issue in and of itself, for different reasons.

Many of these medications are ineffective and the associated side effects and health issues far outweigh any apparent benefits. It is important to intervene and treat this condition early on and for many, depression begins in early childhood, particularly during the adolescent years.

Suppose you examine many of the medications that are prescribed. In that case, you will notice that none of them are advised for children under 18, as they can significantly exacerbate their symptoms.

Over 8% of adolescents suffer from depression in some form and these figures are increasing. The important point is to intervene as soon as possible to prevent them from developing an addiction to antidepressants later in life. Many causes contribute to this disorder in adolescents, including hormonal imbalances, school and family stress and traumatic events.

In the worst-case scenario, it may result in suicide attempts. Many parents who have had to bury their children often wonder how they could have prevented it or what they could have done if they had only recognized the indications. Regrettably, in many of these cases, the signs and symptoms were plain to see.

To begin, there are many indications of depression in children that parents may watch for. The first signs to look for are vague symptoms of physical discomfort, muscle, head or stomach aches or chronic fatigue, persistent difficulties with schoolwork, particularly where none existed previously.

Missing lessons and skipping school entirely are two indicators. Emotional outbursts that occur for no apparent reason include shouting, aggressive behavior, and episodes of crying. If they begin to isolate themselves, lose interest in hobbies and avoid social interactions, these are also indicators of depression.

The issue is that when parents fear their children are depressed, they often minimize the severity of the situation. They also have difficulty facing their children or attempting to be their "friends." Indeed, you should go in the opposite direction and be proactive. While you can discuss these symptoms with your children, you are ultimately the parent and must take charge of the situation.

There are many non-pharmacological techniques to treat depression in children. Occasionally, it is a physical issue that contributes to the overall issue. If your family has a history of bipolar disorder or thyroid difficulties, this may be the underlying problem.

Some tests can determine this and drugs that can help balance hormone levels. These are not antidepressants and if your doctor suggests prescribing them to your child, remind them that there are other options and point them in this way instead.

If your child does not have a physical issue that may be contributing to his or her depression, sit down with them and discuss it.

Make it clear that you are their parents and that you care about their well-being and that you are here to help them if they are acting properly. Adding Omega-3 and Omega-6 fatty acids to their diets, cutting back on processed foods, and making other dietary changes may help.

Spending more time with them, taking them on excursions with you and getting them involved in activities are all-natural alternatives to antidepressants. Therapy provides another avenue for children, as they can confide in an objective third party.

Applaud your teens whenever possible and tell them that you don't mind if they don't always get the greatest grades or win first place in every competition. Do your best to show them that you care about them and really want them to do well. Get a tutor or mentor for them if they're struggling in school.

A wide range of resources and eye-opening facts are accessible on depression and its treatment. You may find a wealth of knowledge on the internet from a variety of sources. To get the most out of these possibilities, do everything you can.

CHAPTER 21

Teen Suicides and Overcoming Hopelessness

Among the biggest causes of death is suicide, regardless of age, gender or ethnicity. In today's youth, suicide is a leading cause of death, accounting for one in three deaths.

As depressing as those statistics are, suicide is one of the top five causes of death among pre-adolescents. Suicide is not amusing at any age but the prospect of someone so young with so much to live for makes it all the more unappealing. Teen suicide is becoming more prevalent worldwide daily.

Many people wonder why such adolescents would take their own lives or what they might be upset about. Many teenagers are under pressure to excel academically, athletically and socially. These ideas can be quite daunting and contribute to feelings of anxiety and tension.

Some adolescents have been abused and neglected and have developed severe depression. Teens who discover they are LGBT and must deal with family and friend rejection are also at risk. Then there are those teenagers who have not received treatment for mental disease.

Teenagers and pre-teens have difficulty transitioning from childhood to adulthood and the world is not always forgiving. Teens are sometimes the toughest on themselves and some are unable to cope.

Because this is not the time in their lives when they communicate with their parents, it is extremely difficult to discern when they are entering a dangerous state of mind. Over half of high school students had considered suicide at some point in their lives.

Over 5% claim to have tried it at least once. This is a genuine cry for help and should never be dismissed lightly, especially if there is no communication in the house and your teenager has nowhere else to go. The next form of communicating and gaining someone's attention is through acting out.

It is important to speak with your teenagers and to observe their behavior. Do not hesitate to inquire about their feelings and assure them that you are there to speak with them when and if they so desire. Many warning signals to keep an eye out for include the following:

- Changes in personality
- Conflicts with pals (girl or boyfriend)
- Isolation and withdrawal
- The standard of schoolwork has deteriorated
- Concentration difficulties
- Choosing behavior that is inconsistent with how they generally behave
- Is this a daughter and if so, is she pregnant?
- Have there been efforts to flee the house?
- Initiate the use of drugs or alcohol
- Physical ailments
- Alterations in eating or sleeping habits

Don't keep quiet if you have reason to believe your adolescent is thinking about harming himself or herself. Talk to them, or someone else. In order to avoid failing you, your teenager will frequently seek advice from a third party.

Ascertain that you are aware of your teen's activities. Concentrate on their words and refrain from passing judgment or becoming enraged. Assure them that you care for them and want them to survive regardless of what happens.

Offer to assist them and be with them throughout their time of need. If necessary, contact your local crisis hotline or an emergency number and arrange for your child to be placed in protective care until they are no longer a danger to themselves.

Whatever you do, do not pretend that nothing is occurring; this could mean the difference between life and death for your child. There are many beneficial programs and drugs available. Early intervention and assistance can result in complete recovery and happy life.

Demonstrate to your child or any child in your life that life is valuable. Inform them not to give up and that assistance is on the way. There is a more hopeful world out there and it is abundant with resources to share.

As adults, we must perceive the dangers around us and assist our adolescents in practically surviving these years of misery. Consider the future and avoid allowing any adolescent to become another statistic. Keep an eye on and listen to your youngsters. It takes more than just words to discern what is truly going on with them.

CHAPTER 22

Receiving Medical Attention for Depression in Children and Adolescents

Depression is difficult to manage as an adult and even more so as a child. Children and even adolescents often struggle to articulate their emotions. Teenagers become moody and retreat from activities as a natural part of growing up. Depression in adolescents is often dismissed as the youngster is a "normal adolescent."

We will discuss some of the indicators of depression in young children and adolescents, behavioral changes that may be observed and how to manage your child. Also, some pointers on how to choose the correct therapist are mentioned briefly.

Four Types of Possible Signs

Signs of Emotion

Sadness - may cry easily, withdraw from family and friends, obsess over little matters and experience bouts of wrath.

Loss of interest - athletes may abruptly stop participating in sports, complain of boredom or refuse to engage.

Worry - they may be tense and fearful; the source of their anxiety may be the reason for their depression.

Cognitive Symptoms (thinking)

Negativity - may be used to put oneself down, as in "I know I'm going to fail."

The child may have a low to a non-existent sense of self-worth.

Worthlessness/guilt - Those fixated on their flaws and failings may exaggerate the severity of those flaws and failures, exhibiting intense guilt and feelings of worthlessness and insignificance.

Hopeless/Helpless - believes that nothing will change and that nothing will improve; that there is no relief from issues (actual or imagined); that things are as they are and that nothing can be changed.

Isolation - withdrawal from family and friends, withdrawal from sports and activities, may spend a lot of time alone in their room, may have suicidal thoughts and/or attempts.

Complaints Regarding the Physical

Weight fluctuations - rapid increase or loss

Sleep changes - either too much or too little sleep and falling asleep at school/class

Slow - may speak, react or walk more slowly; may be less lively or active.

Behavioral Modifications

Avoidance - cessation of contact with family, friends or hobbies

Clinging - may become excessively clinging (desiring to be with one parent or caregiver) and unwilling to let go to participate in activities.

Demanding - they may be adamant about getting what they want instantly.

Restless - fidgety, troublesome at school and impulsive

Self-Injury - may result in self-inflicted pain (burning, cutting themselves)

Receiving Medical Attention

It is important to get help quickly if you feel your child or teen may be depressed. It is important to inquire about their feelings and to converse with them. Introduce children to the concept of chemical imbalance in the brain on their level.

Contact your local mental health organization for more thorough information on assisting your child in coping with depression. Also, your child's physician can provide guidance and information. Psychotherapy or counseling may be required or even recommended.

Medications may be recommended but be aware that antidepressants have been shown to promote suicide thoughts in children as young as age 21. Due to this, your child must be continuously supervised while on medicine.

Also, natural therapeutic options such as herbal supplementation are available. A combination of a specific collection of herbs known to have a beneficial effect on mood and other nutritious components is used to provide the maximum amount of relief from depressive symptoms. The advantage of herbal supplementation is that it has significantly fewer adverse effects if any.

Depression is a difficult illness to manage, even more so in youngsters. What matters is that you seek assistance for them as soon as possible. Also, understand that the

Depression is not your or your child's fault. It is a genuine physical ailment that, for the most part, is easily handled.

CHAPTER 23

How to Motivate Teens

One of our major problems as parents has been how to inspire kids - 2 of our kids in particular. One of them is just plain lazy; the other one is a struggling teenager - troubles in school, often gloomy and at times downright obnoxious.

You need to have a strategy to motivate teens and here are a few suggestions that we've found over the years that we've found work fairly well. We've learned that it's difficult for kids not to be motivated - it just depends on what they're motivated to achieve. Quite often, they're motivated to reject us, retreat or underperform. Instead of acting out, they're behaving in!

So how can you motivate teens?

Here are 3 tips to get you started:

Look at what your youngster likes. The aim here is to observe what your youngster likes to do. Don't take his word for it; he'll say "nothing matters" but look at his actions - does he watch many TV, play video games, play on the computer? Observe and write them down - later on you can utilize these items as an incentive.

Take the sweets out of his room. Underachieving youngsters shouldn't have much in their room - it will merely be a place for them to withdraw.

Put an end to your child performing tasks for you. This is referred to as "learned helplessness," and it is not desirable. It does nothing to assist them in gaining independence.

It is acceptable to assist them in some way, but don't complete their work. They rise to the occasion and are delighted with themselves when I make them do things on their own, which is something I've seen about my children.

One thing to keep in mind is that being an underachiever provides your child a sense of control and power, as she is not concerned with the anxiety associated with failure or meeting duties. Social expectations do not bind her. When individuals begin to anticipate an increase in the number of these children, they disintegrate.

"To be a successful parent, you must prioritize your children's wants and wishes over your own. Bear in mind that it is far easier to develop strong youngsters than it is to mend damaged men."

Parenting may be challenging. These are the common errors made by parents.

Should You Assist with Homework?

Assisting children with their schoolwork may potentially result in a decrease in test performance. Children who receive frequent assistance with their homework do not perform any better than those who do not receive assistance.

Children may even score lower in some situations due to their growing reliance on their parents' intelligence. Punishing children for poor grades is also ineffective. To help children succeed in school, read to them as a youngster and engage them in open discussions about school, life and future ambitions.

Defending your children from failure

Fear of failure is a modern child's "epidemic," and it has a deadly effect. We live in a world of "never good enough," and parents do everything possible to shield their children from failure, which is detrimental. The secret to life success is not to avoid failure; rather, it is to learn from our mistakes and build resilience.

Placing technology and other sources of distraction in bedrooms

Placing gadgets and distractions in a child's bedroom can be hazardous. I know some families who have installed television sets, Xboxes and PlayStations in their children's bedrooms. Children are so sleep-deprived that their grades deteriorate as a result.

They struggle with concentration and focus daily. Perhaps most importantly, they lack any sense of discipline. How are we to forget the brutality inherent in the video/computer games they champion?

Furthermore, what about pornography? Remove gaming consoles, televisions, PCs and laptops, and other distractions to remove the temptation and instill discipline.

Not setting a good example

When it comes to children, parents are the most important role models. Children absorb a lot of information from their parents. Parents should model the type of life they wish for their children.

If you tell a white lie, your child will as well. If you do not cut corners, your child will learn to avoid doing so as well. If you volunteer or make a charitable contribution, your child will emulate you.

Excessive dietary restriction

Parents have very little influence over what their children eat, especially when they are not at home regarding children's eating habits. Since children desire what they cannot have, having too much control over what they eat at home may lead to children picking unhealthy items while they are out. Fast food

restaurants (Pizza and Burger places), soft drinks and a high-fat diet have contributed significantly to children's weight-obesity concerns.

Taking on the role of a friend rather than a parent

In the absence of an authoritative adult, youngsters may make potentially risky choices. Parents need to be parents and not pals during their children's adolescent years.

When children reach the age of experimentation with alcohol (a significant cause of death among adolescents) and drugs, they must have an authority figure and not just another friend. Although being authoritative may not necessarily imply authoritarianism.

Having an excessive amount of say over life-changing decisions

Parents should let their children make their own choices. Allow children to select their own college major. If parents interfere and choose for them, the student will be less satisfied with their schooling.

While voicing your views and sharing your experiences is acceptable, youngsters should be trusted to make informed choices.

Confusion between intelligence and maturity

Because intelligence is often used to determine maturity, many parents believe their children are prepared to face the world when they are not. If a youngster demonstrates giftedness in one area of his or her life, do not assume that skill is evident in all areas of the child's life.

The only way to tell if a child is mature is to look at others their same age. Ensure that your children have a strong feeling of self-responsibility. Maturity is defined as this. It is important for parents to distinguish between intelligence and intellectuality, two terms that are sometimes used interchangeably.

Punishing children for misbehavior

Slapping and hitting are primitive ways of expressing emotions and punishing them can cause youngsters to conceal their emotions. Typically, children act out due to their underdeveloped ability to articulate emotion.

Punishing children for their outbursts may teach them to avoid expressing emotion in the future, even if it is more constructively. Instead of doing this, you should help the child understand and express their unpleasant emotions by empathizing with them.

Conspiracy to compel children to apologize

Forcing children to apologize does not instill social skills in them. It's weird to believe that young children comprehend automatically what they've done and why they need to apologize. If children are coerced into making an apology, it may postpone their natural acceptance of it. Other than that, you should apologize on behalf of your child, setting a positive example.

Safeguarding children from harm and danger

Keeping our children safe may be more harmful than allowing them to play with fire. In the absence of proper knife-handling instruction, how can youngsters be expected to use a knife properly as adults? Because of the sheltered environment they live in, children are unable to learn basic safety precautions.

Parents who spank their children

Physically abused children are more likely to develop mental and personality disorders. "Children who are subjected to physical punishment often develop depression and others develop an addiction to alcohol or narcotics."

Children who are not physically punished - who are not struck or slapped - are much less likely to develop depression or substance dependence. It is important to remember that most adult mental problems can be traced back to physical punishment as a child, demonstrating that spanking has severe and long-lasting consequences.

Constantly reminding their child to stop crying

Telling children to stop crying can obstruct their development of emotional expression. Young children are incapable of expressing their emotions in any way other than via weeping.

How will telling a child "don't weep" make them feel better?

Furthermore, it sends a message to them that their emotions are invalid - and that it is not acceptable to be sad or afraid. Rather than ignoring emotion, you should acknowledge it and assist the child in working through it by teaching them how to express themselves verbally.

Providing youngsters with an excessive number of action heroes and dolls

Excessive exposure to action heroes and dolls has been shown to reduce children's aspirations. With so many professional alternatives available, youngsters who grew up playing with action heroes and dolls saw fewer employment options.

How can Spider-Man, Superman or Iron Man aid in the development of a career?

Will Barbie truly assist?

All these have implausible depictions. Parents should diversify their child's playthings by incorporating books, puzzles, music and different creative games.

Boys being told to "be a man."

Insisting on young boys "man up" or "be a man" can negatively influence their mental health. According to various psychologists, despite its importance in girls' and boys' development, open emotions, compassion, and empathy are often feminized.

This causes many boys to bottle up their feelings, which in some circumstances manifest as violence. Unfortunately, boys and men experiencing mental health difficulties do not seek help, jeopardizing their manhood.

Preserving their children's happiness

Preventing children from experiencing sadness and grief might stifle their emotional development. All parents despise it when their children are unhappy and their natural inclination is to attempt to make things right as soon as possible.

Do not deprive your children of this necessary emotion. If you do, you will be impeding their emotional development. It is important to allow children to experience and master their emotions.

Constantly pressuring children to take "one more bite."

Forcing children to consume additional calories before leaving the dinner table might result in major weight problems. Most parents I know compel their children to overeat, resulting in severe weight issues in their early and older years.

Encouraging children to eat more than they desire also fosters a lifelong dislike for specific meals, such as vegetables, which is the polar opposite of what you want.

Refusing to allow their child to do something

As with forbidden fruit, forbidding your child from doing something or hanging out with another youngster just increases their want to do so. Parents should instead consider what they dislike about the object or child.

Unless the situation is life-threatening, grit your teeth. If they pose a threat to your child, initiate a discussion about values rather than just prohibiting them from doing or seeing something.

Reliance on technology to amuse

Refusing to allow youngsters to overcome boredom on their own can have major implications. There is not just the worry of "electronic addiction," but also the threat that youngsters raised on television would be unable to overcome boredom on their own later in life when they are in school and job. While technology exposure is necessary for today's environment, it should be limited to youngsters.

Excessive admiration for their child

Exaggerating your child's intelligence or athletic ability can scare children away from trying new things. Excessive praise can be restricting, as youngsters will become fearful of trying new things, fearing failure, and losing their status as brilliant. Instead of praising the child's ability, you should emphasize his or her effort; "you're so good at tennis" can become "you always give it your all at tennis."

Submitting a request to be left alone

Consistently telling your children "don't bother me" or "I'm busy" can convey to a child that you feel that way all the time. Children gradually come to believe that communicating with you is pointless. If you do this when a child is young, they may be less likely to confide in you as they get older. Never be hesitant to take a break but never keep your children too busy.

Children - Possibilities

Social difficulties - Withdrawal, loneliness, loss of confidence, school difficulties, learning issues, anxiety and depression, alcohol and drug misuse (especially in conjunction with mental illness), suicide or self-harm, theft and criminal activity.

Selfishness, resistance, unstable behavior, recklessness, deception, violent behavior and disruptive behavior are all examples of discipline problems.

Disruptive conduct, bullying, poor learning ability and academic achievement are all examples of educational issues.

Parents desire immediate resolutions to their child's difficulties, yet the solution is actually within them. I make a concerted effort to present an air of openness and avoid blaming parents for everything.

Still, I seek parents' readiness to fundamentally change their attitudes and behaviors toward their children and engage in meaningful dialogue about their children's future.

CHAPTER 24

Teen Anxiety Coping Techniques

Adolescence can be a difficult time for adolescents as they undergo bodily, psychological and social changes. A combination of both normative and aversive stresses has been linked to an increased risk of internalizing behaviors such as anxiety and depression, as well as the association between culturally diverse youth, stress and at-risk behaviors and various coping mechanisms.

The Regain Your Freedom Technique is one such coping mechanism that, when combined with other approaches such as music therapy, aromatherapy, massage, visualization and daily journaling, assists youth in developing their coping abilities and rehabilitation.

Learning to apply these techniques is a means for them to re-establish their footing. This grounding serves to refocus the mind on the present moment rather than on the previous traumatic experiences linked with anxiety and the family of related diseases.

The trick is not to attempt to erase memories from your mind but to approach them differently.

When enough time has passed and the Regain Your Freedom Technique has been utilized, the triggers that lead teens and adults to return their nervous, anxiety conditions are lessened. The technique has been reinforced in mind by being employed when the initial feelings or memories of worry begin.

While moderate degrees of stressful life experiences are considered a normal aspect of development, elevated amounts can jeopardize children's and teenagers' well-being and healthy development.

Adolescents are exposed to an increased rate of stressful life events. There is evidence that this increased exposure to stressors contributes to the elevated rates of psychological issues associated with this developmental stage.

Many stressful life events and daily annoyances of adolescence are universal for adolescents regardless of their cultural background or region of residence.

The unique cultural-ecological niches that adolescents from diverse cultural groups inhabit as a result of their ethnic group membership and other context-defining factors like their family's socioeconomic status, integration with mainstream and ethnic communities, and neighborhood and school location can pose unique challenges for adolescents from diverse cultural groups.

These elements combine to provide some teenagers with improved opportunities for developing the competencies necessary to become productive young adults. However, these interacting factors often expose teenagers to prolonged adversity and cumulative stressors that overwhelm their anxiety coping mechanisms.

Both lower socioeconomic status and poor health have been associated with stress. This study examines a model that suggests that teenagers from diverse socioeconomic backgrounds differ in their exposure to negative life events and their interpretation of those events.

The study enrolled 100 high school students, roughly half of whom were African American and half Caucasian. Students viewed two distinct videos in a laboratory setting, one of which depicted an ambiguous situation and the other of which depicted a negative situation. Students completed open-ended questions, a questionnaire and their heart rate and blood pressure were monitored.

The findings indicate that adolescents from lower socioeconomic backgrounds are more likely to interpret ambiguous social situations as threatening, implying that interventions to reduce youth threat interpretations may help alleviate the physiological toll associated with these perceptions.

Anxiety coping skills remain the most effective treatment option for assisting a teen in navigating these formative years of development and coping with their changing bodies, psychological and situational experiences.

Many adolescents have already demonstrated improvements in their anxiety coping skills. This technique is simple to use and does not require medication.

Adult guidance and collaboration with teens in implementing this method will also instill a sense of acceptance and support in the teens who require it. We must provide a secure and healthy start for our children to develop into holistically healthy adults.

We must encourage children to engage in regular physical activity and develop healthy eating habits early. This will assist the child in achieving and maintaining a healthy body and mind balance. A healthy body and mind can be achieved through regular exercise. Stress and mental clarity can be alleviated by a healthy diet and frequent exercise.

Assure that the youngster has adequate sleep. While some evidence indicates that teenagers require more sleep than adults, it is often the case that they receive less than they require. Sleep is important for maintaining alertness and attention.

Finally, share the load, provide a safe environment for your child to grow and bloom—home should be a place where children can unburden themselves—listen to your child from an early age, spend quality time with her/him and make her/him feel secure and loved at all costs—don't judge or compare. Bear in mind that each child is unique; ensure that each youngster is emotionally and physically healthy.

CHAPTER 25

Bully-Proof Your Kid - Self Esteem, Stress Management and Bully Solutions Now

It's understandable if you've recently learned that your child has been the victim of bullying, but at least you're privy to the information. As a result, many young people refuse to acknowledge that they are being harassed. In order to prevent bullying, teachers and parents must work together and always be aware of the signs.

Signs to check that your child may be a victim of bullying are:

- Mood swings
- Violent behavior at home\s withdrawal (happy kids don't generally withdraw)
- Sleep issues
- No interest in school\s justifications for not going to school
- Upset/depressed at the notion of returning to school after the weekend\s fear when talking about school\s doesn't talk about any friends or school events

Nothing great to say about school\s appears melancholy or distant\s just seems sad

Various forms of harassment and abuse, such as physical harm, humiliation and humiliation of others, are all forms of bullying. That's exactly how the bully wants your child to see the bully's energy: powerful, overwhelming, and frightening.

160,000 students miss school per year due to bullying. Due of its devastating effect on youngsters, bullying has received widespread attention. On a global scale, bullying is a serious social problem that must not be neglected

Both boys and girls are vulnerable to bullying. Boys, on the other hand, report it less often due to embarrassment. Today, bullying has reached pandemic proportions in the United States of America.

As youngsters get older, the number of bullying victims appears to decrease, as a 2010 study from Clemson University demonstrated. However, older adolescents who have been bullied often endure years of misery. Also, the same study found that children felt unprotected from bullying.

Thus, it is entirely up to us to arm our children with the tools necessary to prevent bullying. Therefore, what tools can we give our children? The following are tactics to employ and ideas to communicate immediately with your children.

1. Maintain a sense of personal space and walk tall. Bullies select their targets based on their perception of easy targets which will make no fuss. They often target persons who do not appear to be armed. If your child does not learn to defend himself, he or she may easily become a victim of bullying.

Walking anxiously with your head bowed and shoulders hunched draws attention and screams out, "I'm not feeling good about myself." Together, practice aggressive body language at home by walking taller and more confidently. Don't allow someone to go too near to your youngster, because this will make him feel smaller than he really is.

2. Take a stand for yourself. It's difficult at times but necessary. 50% of the time, bullying will cease if the victim simply speaks up for himself or herself. Simply inform the bully to halt his or her behavior!

3. Your youngster must develop self-esteem. To accomplish this, he must portray himself confidently, both in his thinking and in his environment. Begin utilizing positive affirmations and nightly positive images to help your child develop a genuine sense of strength, confidence and capability.

Also, nighttime audio relaxations will assist your youngster in better managing stress and anxiety. Consult with your child to ascertain areas in which he feels he could improve. Occasionally, youngsters will say hurtful things. If your child is secure in his identity, he will be less affected by other people's words and attitudes.

Spend time fostering your child's self-esteem. This is importantly important. Bullies target children with low self-esteem. What matters most right now is to begin repairing your child's self-esteem. You can get started right now.

4. Instruct your youngster in the proper use of eye contact with others. Making eye contact demonstrates that you are secure in your identity. Practice at home, when shopping or at the post office - whenever your child has the opportunity to engage in healthy eye contact. Healthy eye contact relates to a healthy sense of self-esteem.

When a child is confident in himself, he will automatically stand taller, make eye contact, initiate nice discussions and advocate for himself. You want to assist your youngster in becoming bulletproof against bullies.

5. Inform the school and faculty of the problem. Teachers and parents should collaborate as much as possible to prevent instances of bullying. Often, teachers are unaware of what is occurring, but students often claim that little or no assistance is provided even when they are.

According to Clemson University research, 30% of males in grades 3-5 and 60% of boys in classes 9-12 reported that their instructor did little or nothing to stop the bullying.

The reality is that many teachers are unprepared to deal with bullying and have no idea how to address it. Regrettably, some teachers are bullied by students.

However, some instructors have received additional training in dealing with bullying concerns. There is always the possibility that your child's teacher will be knowledgeable about dealing with bullying. In any case, discuss the problem with the teacher and school counselor. Inquire about referrals. Do not heed instructions to ignore the bullying. It is ineffective. Children ultimately internalize the sorrow to a greater extent.

Sixth, enroll your child in a martial arts class. Often, it takes only a few weeks for your youngster to develop a new perspective on any bully issue. Today, many martial arts classes incorporate anti-bullying programs, demonstrating a keen awareness of the issue in our society.

7. Take the small things your child says carefully, even if he says them casually. Any threat he may have received should be investigated and handled seriously promptly.

8. If a bullying scenario does not improve within a reasonable amount of time, consider withdrawing your child from school and home educating. As bullying continues to spread across the country, parents must recognize a safe, practical alternative. It is a form of homeschooling.

While home education does involve some structure, it can provide your kid with time to recover and develop her self-esteem while focusing on actual learning. It is lawful in all 50 United States of America and fully removes peer pressure and exam anxiety. Also, it has the potential to eradicate bullying.

This is not to claim that homeschooled children are immune to bullying but are not exposed to it the same way that school-aged children are. Bullying often occurs in the homeschooling context.

Fortunately, in general, homeschooled children have a high sense of self-esteem and self-worth, making them less attractive to bullies. They have an air of competence. Homeschooling does not entail that children must remain at home all day.

Quite the opposite. Cooperatives for homeschooling are sprouting up like ice cream trucks on a summer playground. There, children meet weekly or biweekly to discuss topics of mutual interest. Mothers often teach subjects in which they excelled before becoming Mommy.

When confronted by a bully, home-educated children often easily deflect aggression simply because they are not compelled to remain in situations deemed potentially hazardous to their health.

In this case, a parent does have control over the environment and can monitor interactions and provide immediate assistance when necessary. Homeschooling could be a one-year or two-year solution or become a permanent solution, depending on the family's preferences.

Recently, it has been more usual for middle and high school students to begin homeschooling in response to unresolved school bullying issues. Parents just are no longer prepared to incur the dangers associated with bullying.

9. Understand that bullying is often perpetrated in groups of children rather than by a single child. When this occurs, victims may feel extremely helpless and alone, as if everyone despises them and if it must be their fault if so many children are opposed to them.

Most parents are unaware of the extent of group bullying or its terrible effect on children and adolescents. Recently, as a result of a few parents and educators speaking out in the media, awareness is spreading.

10. Communicate with your child often and always keep the lines of communication open. Allow your child to retreat and do not dismiss it as "adolescence." Your child may be away from you for eight or more hours per day in a school setting.

You may be unaware of what your child is experiencing throughout that time. Stay vigilant and wise; make sure your child trusts you and can count on you to help her and believe her no matter what.

Most people believe that being bullied is a natural part of growing up. That is not the case. We should never threaten, physically injure or emotionally abuse our children. In today's world, things can easily spiral out of control and most children are ill-equipped to deal with the high levels of stress and anxiety that bullying inflicts.

Most parents become aware of childhood stress when their children demonstrate excessive anxiety. This stress must be addressed promptly.

As a parent, one final type of bullying to be wary of is sexual bullying, which is a subtype of sexual harassment. According to University of Illinois professor Dr. Dorothy Espelage, half of all bullying in elementary and middle schools involves LGBT slurs. Sexual bullying occurs in high schools as well.

Sexual bullying is characterized as sexually threatening, intimidating, spreading sexual rumors, making sexual comments or putting them on restroom walls, sending films or SMS or even touching, grabbing or poking the victim. Sexual harassment, which can be directed at any student, also falls under sexual bullying.

All sorts of bullying are detrimental to a developing youngster or adolescent who discovers and defines himself. Act immediately and without delay. Assist your child in developing self-esteem, managing stress and equipping him with the tools necessary to be the very best he can be.

CHAPTER 26

132

Why Treatment is Required for Children with Anxiety Disorders

Children who refused to attend school thirty years ago were believed to be uninterested and lazy. Most parents felt that their children had a "poor attitude" toward school and eventually grew out of it. Psychologists are now reclassifying school phobia as an anxiety disorder that requires early diagnosis and treatment.

Why Treatment Is Required

Experts are asking parents to be mindful of their children's anxiety symptoms to intervene early. Failure to recognize and treat the disease early on may result in poor academic performance, increased anxiety, depression and substance dependence later in life.

Anxiety disorders may impede children from "connecting" with school life; they may also inhibit children from participating in developmental milestone activities appropriate for their age group. By avoiding social interactions at school and elsewhere, children may have fewer opportunities to learn the social skills necessary for adult success.

What Treatment Are Alternatives Available?

A comprehensive study on treatment options for childhood anxiety was done at seven medical institutions in the United States of America. What made this study noteworthy was its objective of comparing various treatment choices for children and adolescents diagnosed with anxiety disorders.

There were three treatment options: a) antidepressant medication, b) cognitive behavior therapy or c) a combination of the two.

According to this study, which involved 488 children aged 7 to 17, 81 percent of children improved with the combination treatment, while 60 percent improved with psychotherapy, which was cognitive behavior therapy, a type of therapy that assists children in confronting children and managing their fears.

Antidepressant medicine benefited 55% of patients. Sertraline (Zoloft), a selective serotonin reuptake inhibitor, as an antidepressant (SSRI). SSRIs work by increasing serotonin levels in brain cells. A placebo group was utilized as a control and improved by 24%. Also, the study's findings indicate that all treatments are safe.

Due to the efficacy of all three treatments, parents have options and choices. Cognitive-behavioral therapy paired with lifestyle adjustments has been shown to have a profound effect on childhood

anxiety problems. SSRIs work by increasing serotonin levels in brain cells. Also, the study's findings indicate that all treatments are safe.

Due to the efficacy of all three treatments, parents have options and choices. Cognitive-behavioral therapy paired with lifestyle adjustments has been shown to have a profound effect on childhood anxiety problems.

What Can Parents Do?

If your child often complains of stomach distress or physical problems before school, you should schedule an appointment with your physician. Take your problem to a specialist and ask for help.

Also, your youngster may exhibit fidgety, clingy behavior for a lengthy period. If this conduct is interfering with your school attendance and performance, contact your doctor.

As we all know, it is not uncommon for teenagers to experience difficulties as they develop and learn. This is entirely typical. However, for some teenagers, their anxiety level rises above the norm, affecting their daily life. These teenagers may struggle with schoolwork, have difficulty forming or maintaining relationships, and avoid social events and activities.

Many of these teenagers will feel pressured to be flawless in every aspect of their lives. This can result in disappointment, as no one is without flaws. It can also be a factor in why some tasks or activities are avoided.

Parents need to monitor their adolescent children for any signs associated with serious anxiety problems. Teenagers are in a unique stage of development, as their psychological makeup is just beginning to take shape for what they will carry into adulthood.

Parents are well aware that teens are often reticent to share their concerns or fears. They may avoid approaching the parent when they are anxious, believing it to be a sign of weakness. As a result, parents must be vigilant for signs of anxiety problems.

The symptoms to look out for include problems sleeping or waking frequently during the night, increased irritability, difficulties at school, mood changes, and sadness.

Parents should also watch for drug or alcohol abuse, as these are often used as a form of self-medication by nervous adolescents. Until shown differently, the use of these substances should be regarded as an indication of anxiety. These substances exacerbate anxiety symptoms, encouraging the kid to use them more often or in higher quantities to make matters worse.

If you believe your teen is experiencing excessive anxiety, sit down and speak with him or her. Encourage the youngster to communicate his feelings, regardless of their nature. Avoid being judgmental since this will likely cause the kid to withdraw. Reassure your youngster that you care and that together, you will find effective treatment choices!

CHAPTER 27

Importance Of Healthy Sleep Patterns For Children And Teens

Sleep hygiene is important for people of all ages. However, developing the proper behaviors early on can save a slew of future difficulties for both of you when it comes to children. Everybody needs a good night's sleep, but it's especially critical for infants and children. Providing your children with adequate sleep is an essential part of being a parent.

Sleeping is among the most vital and pleasurable activities that humans engage in. Awakening refreshed improves the quality of your entire day. It is important for our mental, emotional, and physical wellbeing. Circadian rhythms are governed by light and darkness, although they develop gradually. By six weeks of age, newborns typically begin to develop such sleep-wake cycles.

By the age of two, it has been demonstrated that most youngsters spend more time asleep than awake. Most children will spend approximately 40% of their childhood sleeping. Babies spend around 50% of their time in each of the sleep stages, REM and non-REM. REM sleep accounts for around 30% of sleep by the time a child is six months old.

Newborns sleep an average of 10-18 hours per day. These sleeping intervals might last anything from a few seconds to several hours at a time. Newborns' sleep is disrupted by their need to be changed, soothed, and fed. However, even at this early stage, adopting healthy sleep habits is important.

Babies should be placed to sleep while they are tired, not after they have fallen asleep. According to experts, they will eventually learn to fall asleep on their own. As a parent, it is important to be aware of your baby's sleep cues.

While some babies massage their eyes, others fuss or cry. These indications indicate that they are ready for slumber. Another important element is to acclimate them to circadian cycles by keeping them awake during the day with light and some noise and asleep at night with darkness and silence. This can aid in the promotion of nighttime sleeping.

Nighttime feedings may become progressively unneeded for infants between the ages of 3 and 11 months. By 9 months, 78% of newborns can sleep through the night. Additionally, naps will become less frequent throughout the day.

Again, putting infants to bed when they are sleepy can assist them in developing self-soothing abilities. Establishing consistent daytime and bedtime routines will assist in easing the shift. Making the infant's sleep environment as pleasant as possible will also aid in sleep.

Every day between the ages of two and four, toddlers need to sleep for between 12 and 14 hours. While a daily nap of one to three hours is acceptable for children ages 18 months and older, scheduling it too soon to sleep is advised.

Many children have sleep problems during this stage, including separation anxiety, night anxieties, and/or difficulty getting out of bed as part of their newly acquired independence.

Several suggestions for resolving these challenges include maintaining a consistent bedroom environment, including a consistent sleep schedule. Consistently enforcing limitations and promoting the usage of a security object, such as a blanket or stuffed animal.

Once your child is a preschooler, between the ages of 3 and 5, they typically require between 12 and 13 hours of sleep each night. Children at this age may still have nocturnal worries and consequently have difficulty sleeping.

The same concepts apply here as well. Consistency, a nice setting, and security all contribute to the development of positive habits. As your child grows older, you will be able to explain the important nature of sleep and the need of maintaining a regular sleeping pattern for their health and well-being in greater detail.

Once a child reaches the prepubescent stage, television, video games, the internet, and other forms of media, as well as caffeinated beverages, all have the potential to contribute to sleep difficulties. Providing a peaceful, cool, and dark atmosphere and limiting television and other forms of media, particularly before bed, will all help your child get a better night's sleep.

Teenagers require significantly more sleep than adults. As we age, our sleep requirements decrease. Teenagers, on average, require roughly nine and a half hours of sleep every night, according to the American Sleep Disorders Association.

Most intriguingly, researchers discovered that teenagers require approximately two hours more sleep every night than their eight to ten-year-old siblings. This is in contrast to how parents often organize their children's sleep regimens. Teenagers are frequently allowed to remain up later than younger siblings by their parents.

Teenagers require additional sleep due to their rapid growth rate and hormonal changes. Sleep deprivation at this point can have a range of negative consequences. Inadequate academic performance and mood swings are just two of the most immediate impacts. Sleep deprivation can also contribute to car accidents and depression.

To determine if your adolescent is receiving adequate sleep, look for these typical symptoms. Is your adolescent having trouble waking up in the morning? Is he or she prone to temper tantrums in the afternoons? Does your teen doze off during the day or sleep in excessively on weekends? Is he or she a night owl who has difficulty falling back to sleep?

If you responded yes to any of these questions, it's possible that your adolescent isn't getting enough sleep. Follow some of the ideas outlined above and/or speak with your health care physician about how to begin implementing improved sleep habits.

By adhering to these principles early on, you can increase your chances of avoiding future sleep difficulties.

Sleep hygiene should begin at an early age. However, if you are just getting started, keep the preceding tips in mind. Adolescents are taught about appropriate sleep habits.

Discussing the benefits of sleep with your child will help them understand why you may enforce some less popular restrictions. For example, if you explain to your child that indulging in media before bed can interfere with appropriate sleep, he or she may be more receptive to such advice.

As is the case with smaller children, sleeping areas should be dark, quiet, and welcoming. Additionally, comfortable bedding and a comfortable room temperature are important.

Maintaining a consistent schedule is also important, rather than making up for lost sleep on weekends. All of these strategies will assist children of all ages in developing healthy sleeping habits. We cannot survive without sleep; therefore ensuring that your children receive enough is well worth the effort.

CHAPTER 28

141

Children's Anxiety Therapy

Life was much simpler back then. The children and parents of those shows had no concept of what anxiety was. Perhaps those shows aired before your time. You may recall 'The Cosby Show' and 'Family Ties.' It's clear that the two television generations have vastly different levels of worry, which is reflected in their significant differences in the way they watch television.

What does our era reflect?

Isn't it terrible to consider that our children will grow up to be like 'Stewie Griffin' from the current television sitcom, 'Family Guy?'

Seriously, our children face unique obstacles that no other generation has encountered. Even though our children are maturing at a breakneck pace, they are emotionally incapable of keeping up with the demands.

This is why we continue to witness an increase in youngsters suffering from severe anxiety, stress, violence and depression.

The most recent intervention is anxiety therapy to address our children's concerns, a phrase recognizable to adults, but our children now have access to their professional anxiety therapy coach.

A good anxiety therapy coach has the potential to save your child's life. Indeed, even a poor coach may teach your children vital strategies for coping with school-related pressures from peers and instructors and any worry caused by current events.

Today's youth are confronted with issues years too early. For instance, abusive boyfriends/girlfriends, teen pregnancy or even parenting, sexual orientation concerns, financial difficulties and anxiety about parents splitting are just a few examples.

All too often, we are unaware that these are the factors that contribute to children's worry.

The best advice for parents concerned about their children's anxiety is immediately contact an anxiety therapy coach!

If you are a teen or the parent of a teen son or daughter, you are going through a transition period. We are aware that this is a time of considerable physiological and psychological turmoil for your grown child. According to psychiatrists, parents should grow up with their children to comprehend their wants and aversions.

In most cases, parents blame their children for irresponsible behavior, oblivious to their pasts. These and other more factors contribute to a rebellious attitude among these adolescent children. When he or she is unable to express this attitude, he or she succumbs to depression.

Acute depression- In most cases, adolescent depression is transient or occurs for a brief period and does not signal a significant shift in the adolescent's lifestyle. It could be as simple as exam anxiety, despair in response to an event at school or college, failure in a particular ordeal, a disagreement with a friend, or a girlfriend's breakup.

These are the most common reasons for adolescent depression and typically do not persist for a long time.

Parental discord—Unfortunately, this is a frequent source of adolescent depression. Discord between both parents, the abrupt death of one parent, physical abuse or extreme parental expectations can all contribute to anxiety or depression.

Unawareness of self-change is the stage of life at which a girl or boy endures significant physical and mental changes.

Physiological changes such as attraction to the opposite sex, masturbation and so on can create unneeded tensions among adolescents, all the more so if these themes are taboo at home and school. As a result, adults may become victims of false information and develop feelings of guilt, leading to sadness.

A family history of depression can also cause depression.

Due to one or more of these factors, your youngster cannot evoke positive experiences in life and believes that everything is too horrible here. When he cannot communicate his ideas to his close and dear ones at home, he feels even more isolated from the world. However, if your teen is suffering from recurrent depression, he requires professional care and treatment.

An important component of treatment is family therapy, which focuses on counseling and behavior therapy for both the teen and his or her parents. Also, antidepressant medication may be determined with the assistance of an expert. Teenage is a fleeting state that will never return. Let us make the most of it and take pleasure in life!

Minor concerns are widespread in youngsters but severe anxiety disorders are rare. You must comprehend the distinctions between the two to determine the true nature of the problem and how it can be treated effectively if one exists.

Children are constantly confronted with a plethora of concerns and fears. With time, the children's usual anxiousness also fades away without much effort on their part.

The terror of upcoming exams, the fear of monsters hiding beneath the bed and the panic associated with separation anxiety are all very real to the small children who suffer from them. If the anxiety is a typical case of anxiety, it will subside over time.

When it is necessary to be concerned

Sometimes the fears exceed the normal range and become uncontrollable; this occurs when they have reached a particular level of worry. When this occurs, some may be that the child is suffering from a major illness and is no longer classified as normal.

Many difficulties such as particular disorders, separation anxiety disorders, many classes of anxiety-related problems and social anxiety disorder are fairly prevalent nowadays.

The association of anxiety disorders in America has identified a wide variety of anxiety disorders in many children. We do observe teens who are afflicted by both depression and anxiety concurrently.

If children with this anxiety illness are not treated, they may develop different additional difficulties, including substance abuse, an inability to develop social skills and academic failure.

It is recommended that caregivers, parents and other adults in the vicinity keep an eye out for any changes or signals of worry in the youngsters. Children may attempt to avoid circumstances that make them feel vulnerable or uneasy by isolating themselves and, in some cases, going out of their way to avoid such situations.

It is recommended that parents of children who appear to be suffering from anxiety get expert assistance. This anxiety disorder is easily treatable and, in some cases, cured. This may assist the youngsters in leading a more fulfilling life.

CHAPTER 29

146

Beware Of The Tell-Tale Signs of Teen Depression

There is too much pressure on youngsters today. A few decades ago, childhood meant joy, harmless mischief, games, travel, parents' love and peer connections. Today, all this has changed; today childhood is marked by competitiveness, ambition, struggle for power at home and outside, parents' drive to succeed at any cost, peer pressure to belong and so on.

All this is quite tough on kids who are already fighting to come to grips with the changes in their mind and bodies that occur with puberty and early adolescence. Both girls and boys suffer from different elements - pimples, hair problems, deepening of the voice, breast size, periods, penis size, virginity vs. sex and so forth.

With so much going on, it is not surprising that one in every five youths suffers from one or another form of depression. Can you, as a parent or guardian, notice the indications of teen depression early enough? What are the indicators of teen depression that could help you recognize this problem with your child?

It is often difficult to spot these symptoms or signs because teens are generally defined by odd conduct. However, with a little patience and careful observation you could be effective in spotting the indicators of teen depression, if present.

The first thing you'd notice is that your child has suddenly become a complete slob. Wearing attractively damaged or tattered clothes with crazy hairdos is one thing; wearing dirty clothes, not bathing for days, not combing (or using make-up), and not thinking about what they put on their feet demonstrate that they do not care how they look. This is one very essential indication of teen depression.

Coupled with the horrible appearances you would find that the youngster has no interest in anything they previously liked - music, video games, TV shows, shopping, tormenting their siblings, etc. Nothing is enjoyable anymore and they abandon outside activities (if they ever did), abandon hobbies and prefer to either hide in their rooms or sit in parks doing nothing.

Also, these children's grades have taken a sharp decline. This is one of the most common signs of teen depression and parents virtually always mishandle it. This is because, in their haste to get their children back on track, they would resort to punishment rather than investigating the underlying causes.

Often, parents conclude that their children have lost interest in studying and that their low marks reflect this loss of interest.

Teenagers and young adults are predisposed to anxiety as a result of school-related demands. Teens who suffer from anxiety are stressed out by exams, school activities, peer pressure, and dating or relationship difficulties. Around 13 out of every 100 children and adolescents suffer from some sort of anxiety.

While it is common to feel worried in real-world situations, this is already a condition when excessive worry has no rational basis and stops sufferers from functioning normally in daily life. Teens who suffer from anxiety panic disorder must get treatment immediately, as the disease can progress to other difficulties if left untreated.

This mental illness can result in substance misuse, despair, low self-esteem, bad relationships with peers, recurrent absences and, in the worst-case scenario, he or she may not graduate from high school. If not treated early, adolescents suffering from anxiety disorders may carry the disease into adulthood.

Teens with anxiety disorders often experience episodes of great irrational terror, accompanied by chest pain, pounding heartbeat, shaking, sweating, nausea and a sense of going insane. Teens' unreasonable concerns about ordinary school conditions can interfere with their ability to function effectively in their daily lives.

Although anxiety disorder is the most prevalent mental illness in childhood and adolescents, the good news is that it is curable. If parents detect any of the symptoms mentioned above, it is best to consult a health care expert to obtain an accurate diagnosis. A mental health practitioner who has been educated to work with adolescents who suffer from anxiety can make the appropriate diagnosis.

A melancholy teenager is often difficult to make because simply being an adolescent and growing up implies moodiness that varies from day to day or hour to hour. One thing is some:

Never disregard your teen's out-of-the-ordinary behavior. Frequently, young adolescents and children believe they have no aid or hope and their parents discover this only when it is too late.

Consult your health care physician immediately to ensure that the symptoms they are feeling and the actions you are observing do not indicate a medical problem.

The physician will almost certainly conduct a substance abuse test, as substance addiction can also promote depression. If necessary, a psychiatric evaluation for other disorders such as anxiety, schizophrenia or bipolar disorder will be conducted.

Family counseling is often required when children are involved if risk factors such as a family history of depression, chronic disease, or eating disorders exist.

Typically, an antidepressant is prescribed, such as selective serotonin reuptake inhibitors (SSRIs).

Although these medications act similarly to natural therapies in that they improve serotonin levels, they are not always ideal because they can increase the risk of suicide and suicidal thoughts in children and adolescents.

While these medications have some benefits in specific conditions, they should not be recommended to depressed adolescents. You should discuss with your physician in detail and assess the risks and advantages.

There are many natural remedies for a sad teenager that will help him or her maintain a good emotional balance and attitude. Herbal components can help boost serotonin's neurotransmitter activity, necessary for emotional well-being and normal sleep, energy and hunger levels.

Along with dopamine, another neurotransmitter that helps maintain a balance of good moods and feelings, serotonin adds to our mental alertness and attitude.

Depression is complex and cannot be attributed just to neurotransmitters. However, science has established unequivocally that the hormones in our bodies contribute to different tasks related to our wellness, including emotional wellness.

Self-esteem and confidence also play a significant role in adolescent development and can significantly impact how they handle future stress and obstacles in adulthood. Never disregard your teen's changed habits or attitudes.

Parents should seek treatment for their child to assist him or her in coping with the disorder. Children and adolescents can benefit from a range of treatments, including cognitive-behavioral therapy (CBT), relaxation techniques and medication.

Most importantly, make them feel loved; reassure them that they are not alone and that you are willing to assist them in conquering their anxiety problem. Anxiety disorder is a curable condition that does not pose a threat to one's life. Alternative remedies for anxiety disorders are also a possibility for permanently resolving anxiety disorders.

CHAPTER 30

Suggestions for Depressed Children's Parents

Children and adolescents who are depressed are extremely susceptible and often difficult to manage. Parents and siblings must develop strategies for dealing with them. The following are some strategies that parents, caregivers, siblings and teachers can use to help sad children:

• Educate yourself about depression: Parents should conduct research and educate themselves on depression to spot the early signs of depression. The earlier parents become aware of depression, the better equipped they will be to react and assist their children in dealing with it.

• Parent-child communication: This is possibly the most important activity a parent must engage in to understand their children better. Parents should urge their children to open up and discuss their feelings with them, as hidden thoughts precursor depressive moods. Parental discussions on many themes, such as sexuality, are beneficial even if a child has not been diagnosed with depression.

• Emotional assistance for depressed children: Children who suffer from depression are prone to irritability and easily angered. Most of them find it awkward to speak with or contact their parents about their problems.

Parents should maintain an "approachable face," be calm yet firm and fair, while remaining compassionate and consistent with maintaining control. These youngsters are incapable of handling false allegations and hence it is preferable if a parent is incorrect about any aspect of the child's behavior to accept it.

• Active rather than passive listening: As the proverb goes, "a problem shared is a problem half-solved." This is especially true for depressed adolescents. They do seek attention and attentively listening to them might aid in comprehending their emotions.

Active listening requires a relaxed seating position, continual eye contact, and open-ended questions rather than a simple "Yes" or "No" answer to the inquiry. It is also important to demonstrate an interest in the subject being discussed. This increases the likelihood that the youngster will open up and communicate his or her feelings without feeling emotionally alone.

• Grant children and adolescents their wishes: A melancholy child or adolescent does not behave this way because they enjoy it; inner thoughts and emotions induce their depressed mood.

They require the maximum assistance and hence parents may consider providing them with whatever service they require (within reason). Simply urging them to "bounce back" or "snap out" of their sad states offers them no favors.

• Reassurance and consolation: Depressed youngsters are afraid of their feelings and may feel rejected, worthless, hopeless and bored. Parents must find a method to reassure their children of their support and affection and provide consolation when they are in need. Also, other family members must learn to console these youngsters to help them cope with their pressures.

• Never dismiss a child's feelings: While youngsters are impressionable and naive, their sentiments are just as crucial to them as yours are to you. Any indication of contempt for these impressionable minds can result in terrible consequences, including self-harm and suicide attempts. When children demonstrate or convey their emotions, they should be appropriately interpreted and reacted to.

• Consult a mental health expert: Each seriously depressed kid should have a personal mental health professional, preferably a pediatric psychiatrist, psychologist or certified clinical social worker. This can aid in the detection and treatment of depression in its early stages.

Even if children have access to a counselor or a local therapist in elementary school or college, teenagers may seek these services independently. Still, their parents should join them on their first appointment unless the teenager objects.

A simple exercise to do at home with your child:

If your child becomes unhappy or grumpy on occasion and you believe you might be able to engage him or her in conversation, try the following exercise:

When you are sitting with your youngster, inquire as to which emotion is the most intense at the moment.

"Are you sad or hurt, or how would you define the emotion you are experiencing right now?"

Request that your child gives that sensation a name. It might be the name of a person, an object or simply a ridiculous, odd made-up name. (My acquaintance often refers to himself as "Ebeneezer.") From that point forward, you will only refer to the emotion by its "given name."

Inquire of your child what is attempting to communicate with you. Inquire whether there is anything you (the child) can do to rid yourself of. Encourage your youngster to communicate with his or her "given name" while you are present.

This is a time-consuming and practice-intensive exercise but usually results in a deeper knowledge of the source of the mood or sadness. This activity is not age-specific, although it is significantly more beneficial for non-clinical depression, the type that we all experience on occasion.

It's also worth asking your child if the melancholy or damaged sentiments or despair originate in any part of the body. If they discover that it is in the stomach, for example, any discussion with that "given name" might occur with the child's hand on the stomach. This can be enlightening for a toddler or adolescent to observe that depression always seems to settle in one location on the body.

CONCLUSION

Anxiety and panic disorders afflict tens of thousands of children and adolescents in the United States. I'm grateful if this GUIDE has thrown some light on this issue. We are grateful for your consideration. If left untreated, child anxiety can develop into different anxiety disorders.

Child anxiety can result in different anxiety disorders, ranging from simple adjustment disorders to more severe and debilitating disorders such as panic disorder and post-traumatic stress disorder.

Child anxiety is often accompanied by depression, sadness, withdrawal or irrational fear of dying family members. Child anxiety is extremely common but it is also extremely successfully treated. Before they reach adolescence, approximately 1% to 2% of children suffer from child anxiety.

Suicide risk should be closely monitored. Children who suffer from anxiety disorders are more likely to engage in alcohol abuse during adolescence. Adolescents' co-morbid alcohol abuse/dependence should be assessed and considered when treatment planning for anxiety disorders.

Teen anxiety is a term used to describe a wide range of emotions, including those mentioned above. All adolescents will experience some degree of anxiety at some point in their lives.

Teenagers are often moody. They are often concerned with their appearance, what others think of them and how they interact with others in general but especially with the opposite sex.

The prevalence of anxiety disorders is increasing. It is crucial to understand, however, that anxiety and depressive illnesses are not restricted to adults. Indeed, many children and adolescents develop these distressing and occasionally life-threatening diseases at an early age.

It's rather mysterious why toddlers and adolescents exhibit signs of panic disorder and posttraumatic disorder. However, children and adolescents are not immune to them.

Though there are no statistics on the prevalence of anxiety disorder symptoms in youngsters, the prevalence is rather high in adults (as much as 25 percent in adults). According to some, treating anxiety disorders requires identifying and resolving issues and worries stemming from early events.

Adults often suffer from anxiety and children and adolescents may as well. Occasionally, this anxiety is triggered by traumatic or stressful experiences but the precise stressor is often unknown.

While anxiety disorders are many, the two most prevalent among children and adolescents are Social Anxiety Disorder and Generalized Anxiety Disorder. These children are often anxious and have difficulty in social situations.

Anxiety often expresses itself in very young children as Separation Anxiety Disorder and Specific Phobia. These symptoms often include a strong aversion to separation from caregivers and different seemingly unfounded worries.

Children react differently to comparable anxiety symptoms as adults, which makes diagnosis extremely difficult. Also, it might be difficult to distinguish between a "phase" or rational concern and actual psychopathology. In any instance, it can significantly impair a child's sense of well-being and academic progress.

According to Chris Burke, school liaison at The Guidance Center in Franklin, Tennessee, Untreated anxiety can result in social isolation and melancholy. Once diagnosed, your physician may be able to assist you, either with or without medication. The symptoms could also be a side effect of another drug your child is taking.

Anxiety disorders can be diagnosed by observing your child's behavior at school. People who see your child on a regular basis can be a good source of information.

If your child's teachers observe similar behaviors, discussing your concerns with a physician would be prudent. With information from all parties, he or she will be more equipped to make an accurate diagnosis.

It is safe to treat anxiety disorders in youngsters. It is significantly more successful when combined with appropriate and consistent health care. Many anxiety disorder symptoms that may emerge in a child include intense fear, cautious conduct, stress manifestations and worrying.

Many people display these habits even when they are not experiencing difficulty. However, the important point here is to comprehend the individual's true level of reactivity in some situations.

There is a healthy level of such behaviors and an extreme and problematic level of such activities. Also, it is important to understand that worry affects a person (particularly children) in two ways.

One is manifested physically, while the other is manifested emotionally. Physical symptoms may include nausea, headaches, numbness in the hands and even sweating. Children, on the other hand, can be emotionally affected, which manifests as fear or uneasiness.

It is important to address such concerns early on so that the child's experience of the world - whether internal or external - is not distorted by an anxiety condition. If he is not given adequate attention, his fundamental understanding of the universe, society, relationships and even his physical reactions may be harmed.

Anxiety and depression disorders are severe and important issues that must be addressed. It is important to pay close attention to them before dismissing a child's or a teen's conduct as typical adolescent tantrums. This is among the simplest ways to leave a youngster or adolescent emotionally (and physically) distraught.

On the other hand, a support system is one of the most effective strategies to assist an individual in overcoming such conditions. Any guardian or parent who cares for a child or adolescent should be expected to provide proper support.

I hope this book has helped the reader understand the alarming rise in the prevalence of childhood and teenage mental health issues. I beg you to seek quick care if you suspect that your child has an anxiety-related mental disorder based on the information in this book.